GOD, AND THE

By Dr. J. Calvin Alberty

Dr. J. Calvin Alberty's
God, and the Mind-of-Man Connection

Food and the Fall: The Adam and Eve Syndrome

Wijah Publishing

Dr. J. Calvin Alberty

First Edition

DR. J. CALVIN ALBERTY'S

GOD, AND THE MIND-OF-MAN CONNECTION

Food and the Fall: The Adam and Eve Syndrome

WIJAH Publishing Company, LLC

wijahpublishing.com

All rights reserved. No part of this book may be reproduced or transmitted in any form or by any means, electronic or mechanical, including photocopying, recording or by any information storage and retrieval system, without written permission from the author, except in the case of brief quotations embodied in critical articles and reviews.

Unattributed quotations are by Dr. J. Calvin Alberty
Copyright © 2015 by Dr. John C. Alberty
ISBN 978-1-940-525-15-0
First Edition
Printed in the United States of America

Library of Congress Cataloging-in-Publication Data

Alberty, John
God, And The Mind-of-Man Connection
by Dr. J. Calvin Alberty. – 1st ed.

Includes bibliographical reference
Cover image designed by Troy Everett Creative

By Dr. J. Calvin Alberty

Table of Contents

Chapters	TITLE	PAGE
	Table of Contents	4
	About the Author	7
	Acknowledgements	9
	Dedications	11
	Warnings and Disclaimers	13
	Preface	14
1	From Heaven to Eden	17
2	The Brain	27
3	The Most Special Function of the Brain	33
4	The Assault of the Enemy Against the Brain	37
5	God, and the Mind-of-Man Connection	45
6	Beginning a New Mindset	49
7	Two Ways and Six Doors	51
8	Guard Well the Avenues of the Soul	67
9	Weak and Enfeebled Minds (Mind Seduction)	77
10	Appetite	81
11	Our Belly as God	83

Table of Contents

Chapters	TITLE	PAGE
12	The Starved and Dizzy Brain	87
13	The Tremendous Power of the Mind	91
14	The Reciprocal Nature of the Mind and Body	97
15	Really Beginning a New Mindset	101
16	The God Given Power of Choice	105
17	The Subconscious / Unconscious Mind	109
18	Do We Have Control or Not?	111
19	The Structure of the Mind	121
20	Other Factors contributing to Loss of Control	127
21	The New Mindset of Mind Control	133
22	Three Ways We Believe and Hold onto Things	139
23	A New Mindset Conclusion	149
24	Wisdom	161
25	Notes	167
26	References	168

By Dr. J. Calvin Alberty

About the Author

Dr. J. Calvin Alberty is a Licensed Professional Counselor in the State of Georgia. At the time of this publication, he also has the following credentials: Nationally Certified Counselor; Master Addiction Counselor; and Clinically Certified Juvenile Treatment Speicalist. He holds a doctorate (Ed.D.) in Counseling Psychology as well as a Ph.D. in Nutrition from a holistic perspective.

Dr. Alberty is passionate about the rich and beautiful, and sometimes overwhelming experiences bestowed upon him by God. They have been both good and not so good. His writings are the reflections of a life lived believing that God is good and faithful. He shares these experiences in a most powerful and authentic way. There is passion and fire emanating from his love of truth, with which God has blessed him to know and share. He is thankful that you have this book in your possession. He is prayerful that you will read, enjoy, study and embrace the truths revealed in its pages. Please share it with others. In fact, definitely share it with others. The Bible says that there is a time and a season for everything under the sun. Now such a time has come for the birth of this book. It is time once more for another authentic voice to speak what God has shared with him. You will now become the recipient of what has been revealed to this author. May the blessings of truth attend you; the voice of reason keep you; and the wisdom of God forever lead you.

Dr. J. Calvin Alberty

Acknowledgements

Thanks to my dear wife of more than 42 years (Evelyn) for the great commitment that she demonstrates in seeing every book through to the end. It is her indefatigable encouragement and love that has, each step of the way, become the wind beneath my wings. I would like to acknowledge the inspiration that others have given. I am thankful to Dr. David Moore who has been inspirational in providing the initial venue from which the ideas and thoughts for this book were presented.

I express gratefulness and gratitude to my mother, Dorothy Burton, who has passed through this life to rest and wait for the return of Jesus. She abides still in my memory with her ever comforting prayers of faith and support. I am aware of the future challenges for little Jay and Jordan, who I greatly desire to leave a legacy of love and authenticity. I acknowledge the great influence of my grandmother Elizabeth Davis Lewis. Her love was greatest when I needed

By Dr. J. Calvin Alberty

it most. This, along with my love for Kim, John, James, and Corey motivates me to work through the weariness and even exhaustion.

I acknowledge that the most important factor in making this book possible has been the love and care of an awesome God. He is a God who specializes in making a way out of no way. Finally, thanks to Vincent, my genius brother, who taught me the value of laughter.

Dedication

This book is dedicated to the South Atlantic Conference Health Retreat. What an amazing display of spirituality, brilliance and planning. It applauds those who do not readily accept what they see and hear as facts without healthy skepticism and inquiry. These individuals go beyond the surface appearance and investigate. They are not impressed by someone's popularity, how many books they have authored, degrees earned, wealth amassed, what they drive, where they live, who they hob-snob or rub shoulders with, or even how widely they are admired by a paparazzi like following.

These individuals are unimpressed by anything other than the truth. They are fact gatherers. They are observant and even skeptical. They do not just say, "That sounds about right." No, these individuals to whom I dedicate this book, will dig down to the root of issues and uncover the deep hidden matter and sustenance of life.

By Dr. J. Calvin Alberty

I challenge you to become one of them, and not only expand your view of life on this earth, but expand your view of life to include the heavenly, new earth, and eternal existence that await those who truly love God. I dedicate this book to these investigators and lovers of truth! I dedicate this book to the success awaiting them. I dedicate this book to their unlimited possibilities and what those possibilities might mean to others as they change the world. They are the ones who ask, not what is, but what could be. Dear reader, I dedicate this book to YOU!

Warnings and Disclaimers

This text should be used only as a general source of enjoyment and inspiration. This book and no other book is intended to replace common sense and wisdom. The purpose of this book is to share with you the power of thought, thinking, and the choices and decision-making that comes to fruition as a result of that thinking.

You are unique and you must find your own voice. Your voice must be authentic, genuine, and true. You will find your true voice coupled with your passions. You must consistently make empowering and life enriching decisions for your life.

The author, Dr. J. Calvin Alberty, and WIJAH Publishing Company, LLC shall have no liability or responsibility to any person or entity with respect to any loss or damage caused, or alleged to have been caused, directly or indirectly, by the information contained in this book.

By Dr. J. Calvin Alberty

PREFACE

LET ME SHARE A PIECE OF MYSELF

There is no choice that you will make in your life that will be as important as the ones that will affect your eternal destination. Such is the contemplation of this book. This is not about a church. It is not about what your mother, father, teacher or pastor has to say or have said. This is about you. This is about eternity. This is about the children who will look at you and want to model your behavior and life.

You only control your life if it is yielded to God. I know that this sounds like an oxymoron, but none the less, it is the truth. Though no individual should have control over the life of any other adult, they can have a sphere of influence that can have a profound impact on those who receive the love and care that emanates from them.

Truly, you are always communicating to others when you are in their presence. Do you know what you are communicating? Whether you are doing this verbally or non-verbally; you are doing it. Be aware of who you are, whose you are, what you are communicating, and the destination of the road upon which you are traveling. However, you should be especially aware of the destination at the road's end.

I believe that every soul has been called into existence for a purpose. The time is far spent, and the God of Creation and eternity is calling you to your purpose. Your mind must be clear so that you can discern or hear His voice. You will hear Him tell you that you have been called for greatness. However, not as the world sees greatness, but as God sees it.

There is a definitive purpose for your life. This book does not attempt to make any choices for you. It does however, desire that you will be able to make your own choices. It also wants you to be acutely aware of the fact, that there are real forces attempting to take that power from you. It is our desire to open your eyes to this reality, so that you may guard well the avenues to your mind. This is where the thief tries to break in and take control of your life.

By Dr. J. Calvin Alberty

From Heaven to Eden

How did it come to pass, that in a perfect creation, among beings that were flawlessly created (Ezekiel 28:15); one could become a devil? Even more so, how could this be the case when his creator loved him beyond human comprehension? How could this be when he was given the highest position in heaven of any created being? He was the covering cherub that stood in the direct presence of God (Ezekiel 28:14). How could this be when he was (Ezekiel 28:12) created full of wisdom? How could this be when he was (Ezekiel 28:12) created in perfect beauty? How could this be when he was talented beyond description? The Bible says in Ezekiel 28:13 that his tabrets and pipes were prepared in him the day that he was created. These are musical instruments that Merriam-Webster online dictionary says are "played by the same person."[1]

This angel had everything above all angels. He was created perfectly, highly loved, extremely talented, held the highest position of a created being, full of wisdom, and perfect in beauty. There was nothing else that God could give him, but still, impossible as it seems, he wanted more.

This created being allowed the seed of iniquity to spread its dark and deadly roots and tentacles within him, until (Ezekiel 28:15) iniquity was found in him. Now, this once perfect angel stood in defiance and in direct opposition of an all-powerful God; a God who could have vaporized him in a nano-second.

He rebelled to the point that Revelation 12:7 says that there was a war in heaven. The results of that war, which is found in Revelation 12:9 says that "the great dragon was cast out, that old serpent, called the Devil, and Satan, which deceiveth the whole world: he was cast out into the earth, and his angels were cast out with him."

Can you believe that? Satan's evil influence was so pervasive and ubiquitous until it contaminated one-third of the angels in heaven. These angels made a conscious and well contemplated choice to follow Lucifer (Satan) in his rebellion against our Creator God who is pure love.

Satan and his angels were cast out of heaven and to the earth; and a cry came forth saying, "Woe to the inhabiters of the earth and of the sea! For the devil is come down unto you, having great wrath . . ." Now, here on earth, Satan finds himself in the beautiful and unstained Garden of Eden. He is confined to the tree of knowledge of good and evil. God had created man on the sixth day of creation. God had made man upright and in God's own image. The sinless couple had been warned of God to stay away from the tree of knowledge. They had been created to the glory of their creator God. They had to have known of His great love, and that He would never tell them anything that was not for their own good.

Let's pause here for a moment and give consideration to at least two physical structures of man upon his creation. Return with me to Eden on the day of man's creation. Can you imagine God on the sixth day as He prepared to make man? Everything that He had done relative to the creation of the earth was in preparation for man's creation. Let's first

By Dr. J. Calvin Alberty

look at it from a modern day comparison of preparation, and then we will return to Eden.

Imagine that you can see a young couple expecting their first child, which is to soon enter the world. They painstakingly day-by-day prepare a special room in anticipation of the child's arrival. All tests reveal that it will be a son that they will be blessed with. They know and are excited about the grand day of the expected birth. They realize that much is yet to be done to ready the home for their first and only child.

They purchase a crib for the baby, along with a playpen, clothes, bottles, and many other things. The big day arrives. As they prepare to head off to the hospital, the young couple pauses to take a last look at the baby's room.

They have been doing everything that they could think of; even baby monitors and storybooks are awaiting the child's arrival. They have made their home a warm and inviting place that will provide a safe, secure and protective environment for the newborn.

The truth is that this couple did the same thing that our ever-considerate Heavenly Father did in preparation for man's creation and placement into his new Edenic home. Let's listen to what Isaiah says in regards to God's thoughtful creation of the earth. In Isaiah 45:18 we find, "For thus saith The Lord that created the heavens; God Himself that formed the earth and made it; He hath established it, He created it not in vain, He formed it to be inhabited....."

Do you hear that? It says that God formed the earth to be inhabited. Listen, it says, He did not form it in vain, He formed it to be inhabited by man. Notice that God did not just form the earth to be inhabited by man, but Genesis 1:26 says that man was to have dominion over every living thing that moveth upon the earth.

Isn't it wonderful how our great creator and loving God does everything with a noble and holy purpose? So the environment was at last ready. Now, from the very dust of the earth God forms man into His own image, Genesis 1: 27.

By Dr. J. Calvin Alberty

He then places the man Adam, from whom He later makes Eve, into his perfect Edenic home, Genesis 2:8.

Isn't it amazing, that when we see birds building their nests, foxes digging their holes, and bees constructing their hives, in preparation for their young, we seldom think of how God did the very same thing for us.

Think about it. The birds do not build flat nests because the eggs might roll off or the young hatchlings might fall from the nest. Foxes keep their young pups underground to protect them from the elements and predators. The bees build hives and are armed with painful stingers to protect the inhabitants of their hive.

Ponder for a moment, how it is all about nurture and protection. All of these structures are designed to protect their inhabitants and provide a safe place for nurturing them. When it came to man, God created him a pure, safe and sinless world. It was a beautiful and majestic garden. It was safe and serene until Satan was cast out of heaven onto the earth, as we mentioned earlier in regards to Revelation 12: 7-9.

Remember also what we said about Revelation 12:12? It says "Woe to the inhabitants of the earth... for the devil is come down unto you, having great wrath...."
My acronym for this "Woe" is **W**atch **O**ut **E**verybody.

Watch out because the devil has come down as a potential avenue for sin to infect humanity. We all know the rest of the story of Adam and Eve and their perfect home. However, it is now time to speak on those two structures that I mentioned earlier when I said, "Let's pause here for a moment and give consideration to at least two physical structures of man upon his creation." Now is the time that I want to briefly focus on those two structures.

Those structural parts of Adam that I am speaking of is the design of Adam's head. Yes, I said the design of Adam's head. Bear with me. It will only take a brief moment.

My initial question arises from the observation of the skull. It is a bony structure apparently designed to protect Adam's

By Dr. J. Calvin Alberty

and all of mankind's brains. Notice that this particular structure encapsulates almost the entire brain as does no other structure in the body. The question that this observation gives rise to is, "What is so important or unique about the brain that God would place such a covering around it?"

My second question is about the structure of the brain. "Could it be that the brain is so delicate, so important, and so complex that it actually requires this special protection?" Could it be for these reasons, as well as others, that the brain might be a much deeper issue than we are aware of?

Let' take a look at the brain and its home. Yes, I say home, because the skull is a place where the brain is nurtured and protected. I know that this might be a radical notion, but open your mind and contemplate this view. Remember, Thomas Dewar says, "Minds are like parachutes. They only function when open." So open your mind and come with me as we investigate our next question.

Remember however, that any good research will always give rise to more questions. The good thing is that additional questions should logically generate more answers. So let's move forward.

By Dr. J. Calvin Alberty

The Brain

My next question is, "Could it be that God knows much better than we do, the delicate nature of our very complex and special brain?" Surely He does. There is this elusive and mysterious component of the brain that regardless of what any man says, the truth is that we do not fully understand it. It is the mysterious and elusive essence of what we call the mind.

The brain is the core, center, and pith of everything that we are or claim to be cognitively. It is the seat of intelligence, the processor of all sensory input, the place where all thinking, reasoning, emotions, and thoughts take place. However, somewhere within it, and there are many theories, lies the mind. Here are some interesting brain facts:

- The human brain is the largest brain of all vertebrates relative to body size[2]
- It weighs about 2.8 to 3 pounds[2,33,4]

By Dr. J. Calvin Alberty

- "Your brain is 2 percent of your body's weight but uses 20 percent of your oxygen supply and gets 20 percent of your blood flow."[5]
- The cerebrum makes up 85 percent of the brain's weight.[6]
- It contains billions of nerve fibers (axons and dendrites), the "white matter"[7]
- These neurons are connected by trillions of connections, or synapse. "The Human Connectome Project ... hopes to map the brain structure--all 86 billion nerve cells and 100 trillion connections that are estimated to make up the neural pathways."[8]
- The human brain is the command center for the human nervous system. It receives input from the sensory organs and sends output to every part of the body
- It's often said there are 10,0000 miles of blood vessels in the brain when in fact that number is

closer to 400 miles, which is still a significant number.[9]

- Over 140 proteins in the brain are negatively impacted by exposure to electromagnetic frequencies—the kind emitted by your cell phone, electronic, and other electrical devices.[10]

- The average number of thoughts that human are believed to experience each day is 12,000 to 50,000 or 50,000 to 70,000 and 70% of them are believed to be negative.[11]

- Your brain is 73% water. It takes only 2% dehydration to affect your attention, memory and other cognitive skills.[12] "This organ is very sensitive both to a deficit in water and to an excess.[13]"

- More than 100,000 chemical reactions take place in your brain every second.[14]

- Between 2013 and 2015, Japanese scientists have carried out the most accurate simulation of the human brain up to now. The researchers successfully managed to model a single second's worth of activity from just one percent of the brain taking one of the world's most powerful supercomputer 40 minutes to calculate

- 25% of the body's cholesterol resides within the brain. Cholesterol is an integral part of every brain cell. Without adequate cholesterol, brain cells die.[15]
- We are NOT getting smarter. Since the Victorian era, average IQs have gone down 1.6 points per decade for a total of 13.35 points.[16]
- Our attention spans are getting shorter. In 2000, the average attention span was 12 seconds. Now it's 8 seconds. That's shorter than the attention span of the average goldfish, which is 9 seconds.[17]
- Brain cells cannibalize themselves as a last ditch source of energy to ward off starvation. So in very real ways dieting can force your brain to eat itself.[18]

- A piece of brain tissue the size of a grain of sand contains 100,000 neurons and 1 billion synapses all communicating with each other.[19]

The reality is that I only mentioned these few points or brain facts to speak to the issue of the amazing complexity of the brain. There is an infinitely greater portion not written about the brain. I truly believe that the undiscovered knowledge of the brain's mysteries, secrets, and complex workings could fill innumerable volumes of textbooks.

The little that is written here, is for the purpose of saying, that as man progresses in his knowledge of this very complex organ, he will discover that we know **far less** about the brain, than we, in fact, actually know about the brain.

By Dr. J. Calvin Alberty

The Most Special Function of the Brain

Now let's turn our attention back to why it is so important to protect the brain. The main reason can be found in this quote by Mrs. Ellen White.

I do need to pause here and share with those of you who are unfamiliar with her, the following biographical sketch that was taken from the White Estate's website. "In brief, she was a woman of remarkable spiritual gifts who lived most of her life during the nineteenth century (1827-1915), yet through her writings she is still making a revolutionary impact on millions of people around the world. During her lifetime she wrote more than 5,000 periodical articles and 40 books; but today, including compilations from her 50,000 pages of manuscript, more than 100 titles are available in English. She is the most translated woman writer in the entire history of literature, and the most translated American author of either gender."[20]

Ms. White writes, "The mind controls the whole man. All our actions, good or bad, have their source in the mind. It is

By Dr. J. Calvin Alberty

the mind that worships God and allies us to heavenly beings.[21]

Another interesting quote by Mrs. White is "The brain nerves which communicate with the entire system are THE ONLY" (all capitalizations of this nature is provided by the author of this book for the purpose of emphasis only) "medium through which Heaven can communicate to man and affect his innermost life. Whatever disturbs the circulation of the electric currents in the nervous system lessens the strength of the vital powers, and the result is a deadening of the sensibilities of the mind."[22]

Did you get it? Did you hear that? The mind is what we worship God with. Not only do we worship God with our mind, but the mind is the only medium through which God can communicate with man.

Do you get it? I mean do you understand what these two quotes are saying when combined together?

THE MIND WORSHIPS GOD, AND IT IS THE ONLY THING THAT GOD USES TO COMMUNICATE WITH US.

Stop reading and really ponder on this. Think about it please. Because the mind is the ONLY place where God communicates with us, and the place where we worship God. This makes it an issue that is connected with salvation.

It is sad to say, but many of us do not get it. If only for this single solitary reason alone, (the mind being the place of worship and the only point of communication with God) the mind must be highly regarded, treasured, and protected by man. Though I plead with and even beg mankind to esteem his mind as sacred; I know that man cannot respect, protect, guard, or begin to value what he does not recognize or sense as extraordinarily sacred.

It is sacred because this is where God meets with man and where man meets and worships God. If we consider the division of the sanctuary of old in the camp of Israel and that which Solomon built, and likened our body temple to it, then our mind would be the Most Holy Place or the Holies of Holy.

By Dr. J. Calvin Alberty

The Assault of the Enemy Against the Brain

And while most men remain ignorant of the mind being the only medium through which God communicates with Him; we must ever realize that on the other hand, Satan, the Bible says, in Ezekiel 28:12, is full of wisdom.

Now let me ask you a question. Do you think that Satan, who is full of wisdom, might know how delicate the human brain is? Do you think that it is even possible that he might know how important it is relative to man's salvation?

Do you think that Satan, who goes about as a roaring lion (1Peter 5:8) seeking whom he may devour, will take note of this information? Do you believe that Satan, who goes about as a thief according to John 10:10 "to steal, and to kill, and to destroy" will not take full advantage of this information? Do you think that there is even the slightest possibility that this diabolical and foul being, who is supremely evil, will not exploit this knowledge to destroy you? By "this knowledge," I am referring to the issue of the mind being the ONLY point of

By Dr. J. Calvin Alberty

communication from God to man, and the hallowed point at which man worships God.

Do you think that Satan, who desperately desires worship, knowing that man worships God with his mind, will not do everything within his power to attack that mind? Consider this, if you were the enemy of God and,

1. If you were full of wisdom

2. And you knew that the only way that God communicated with man was through his mind, which we will call, "God, and the Mind-of-Man Connection."

3. And you knew that apart from God man was helpless; then what would you do? What would be the focal point of your assault? The logical answer has to be "THE BRAIN." How soon would you begin your assault on the brain? Would it begin prior to conception, in the womb, during the delivery, or after the birth? Or would it be all of the above?

The answer is so obvious that none of us should be surprised to find that this is all of the above. Yes, this is exactly what the enemy of souls has done. The enemy's assault on the brain begins before we ever breathe our first breath!

This is why preconception health practices are so important for parents-to-be. Imagine the assault against the genetic carriers of those who are child bearing age. The enemy does everything he can to damage their DNA and condemn them to poor health.

The Center for Disease Control says, "Preconception health refers to the health of women and men during their reproductive years, which are the years they can have a child. It focuses on taking steps now to protect the health of a baby they might have sometime in the future."[23]

Detrimental factors can include, but are not limited to "tobacco use, alcohol use, inadequate folic acid intake, obesity, hypertension, and diabetes."[24] Other factors can include inadequate nutrition, infections, mental and physical abuse before conception, stress, anxiety, depression, and frequent mental distress.[25]

By Dr. J. Calvin Alberty

During pregnancy is another time that the enemy seeks to damage the unborn child. This can occur because of prescribed medications, illegal drugs, poor or altered nutrition, maternal stress, alcohol or tobacco used by the mother during pregnancy, certain infections or vaccinations, chronic conditions such as diabetes, and not seeing a health care provider regularly.

All of these can be an assault on the prenatal infant's brain. Assaults on the brain also occur during a child's effort to just leave the womb at birth.

Possible causes of injury during delivery are:

1. Umbilical cord tied around the fetus

2. Use of forceps to assist the delivery

3. Failure to breathe

4. A breach of the child or some similar condition, and . . .

5. Incompatible Rh proteins between the child and mother.

There are also the possible causes of injury to the brain after the birth and the development of the child over the life span. However, these are just too numerous to mention any more than just a few such as: mind altering illegal drugs, prescription-based psychotropic medications, stress, alcohol, depression, physical, mental and emotional trauma, environmental agents, brain disease, strokes, and brain aneurysms.

When I said that the number of mental disorders were too numerous to list, I really meant it. All you have to do is take a glimpse into the Diagnostic and Statistical Manual of Mental Disorders, Fifth Editions (DSM-V). It will quickly reveal to you exactly what I mean. In the fourth edition of this book (DSM-IV), there are over 900 pages of mental disorders with their diagnostic criteria, features, specifiers for types of disorders and their subtypes. Notice, in the few disorders that are listed, there is an intimate connection of body and mind. When reference is made to the mind negatively affecting the body, it is speaking of the actual physical person. What their mind is perceiving, or thinking, could physically alter their vital signs and affect their behaviors.

By Dr. J. Calvin Alberty

Those vital signs could be manifested as an elevated or rapid heart rate, difficulty breathing, manic or depressive behaviors, pacing, profuse sweating, crying, etc. The disorders or conditions that follow below, as you will note, have an intricate connection between the body and mind. In essence, many of these mental disorders have behavioral components that are expressed as odd, unusual or strange behaviors. Here are a few disorders listed in the DSM-IV:

Alcohol/Substance abuse (affects mind and body)

Anxiety Disorders (affects mind and body)

Bipolar Disorder (affects mind and body)

Depression (affects mind and body)

Generalized Anxiety Disorder (affects mind and body)

Obsessive-Compulsive Disorder (affects mind and body)

Panic Disorder (affects mind and body)

Posttraumatic Stress Disorder (affects mind and body)

Schizophrenia (affects mind and body)

Social Anxiety Phobia (affects mind and body)

Sleep & Wake Disorders (affects mind and body)

Nightmare Disorder (affects mind and body). [26]

You were asked earlier to notice the mind and body connection associated with mental disorders. The reason for this will be explained later. However, for now you are to just think about the fact that there are more than 900 pages in a book listing mental disorders dealing with mankind. Now in light of all of the mental disorders of the mind, do you think that Satan has effectively done, and is successfully doing his job of attacking the mind of man?

By Dr. J. Calvin Alberty

God, and the Mind-of-Man Connection

Have you begun to see the big picture? Have you grasped the fact that there is an all-out assault against the brain of man by Satan? Are you now at least beginning to think that just maybe the mind/brain is very important? It has to be critically important for Satan to begin his attack on it even before birth. As if that is not enough, he continue this attack throughout man's life-span and does not relent until man has met his death?

If the brain or mind was not vital, why would he be so aggressively doing what he is doing against it? Remember, good research or investigations generate more questions.

Satan is committing this all-out, unabashed, blatant, and shameless assault because he knows what Ellen White says is true. She writes in the book Child Guidance, "The brain nerves which communicate with the entire system are THE ONLY medium through which Heaven can communicate to man and affect his innermost life."[27]

By Dr. J. Calvin Alberty

This statement is so very important that you will see it mentioned repeatedly. The brain nerves which are the ONLY medium through which Heaven can communicate to man; is henceforth denoted as "God, and the Mind-of-Man Connection."

Here is where we must begin constructing a new mindset. It is a mindset that deals primarily with an intense awareness of what is transpiring before our very eyes and far too many of us are blind to it. It is reminiscent of a church spoken of in the third chapter of the book of Revelation. The statement is rendered in verse seventeen. "Because thou sayest, I am rich, and increased with goods, and have need of nothing; and knowest not that thou art wretched, and miserable, and poor, and **BLIND,** and naked.

Do you see that they did not see their condition? They said that they were rich, increased with goods, and needed nothing. They said this even though the truth was very much to the contrary. Laodicea was in fact, wretched, miserable, poor, naked, and **BLIND**. The saddest part of this is not that they were blind. The saddest part is that they did not know that they were blind. How can you be blind and do not know it?

I guess a lot of individuals will find out on the Day of Judgment when they hear the rebuke of Christ after they cry out to him saying, "Lord, Lord, have we not prophesied in thy name? And in thy name have cast out devils? And in thy name done many wonderful works?" And they will hear Jesus say unto them, "I never knew you: depart from me, ye that work iniquity" (Matthew 7:22). How could these people have been so deluded about their spiritual condition and the status of their relationship with Christ?

Those spoken to in Matthew 7:22 were in the same condition as those individuals were in the church of Laodicea. Sadly, their condition was killing them both. How could they believe that they were alright with God, when in actuality they were so far from Him? Something tells me that they must have either separated themselves or allowed

Satan to separate them from "God, and the Mind-of-Man Connection."

This is the primary purpose of Satan's efforts. He desires passionately to prevent, break, or distort the "God, and the Mind-of-Man Connection" that exists in the brain or mind. Satan does this so that:

> We will no longer recognize or know God's voice
>
> We do not discern what is important to God
>
> We live in confusion, of which God is not the author
>
> We turn our attention to the world, away from God
>
> We cannot distinguish the holy from the unholy
>
> We are lost, as our minds are dulled to the point that we are no longer feeling a need for God in the important parts of our lives, such as our health and our spiritual status with Christ.

Beginning A New Mindset

So with this understanding, let's look DEEPER into really beginning a new mindset. This means looking into guarding and protecting our minds from the enemy's all-out, perpetual and fatalistic assault. Before we do this however, it is important that an earlier quote is repeated. It is the one that I mentioned would be repeated over and over again.

"The brain nerves which communicate with the entire system are THE ONLY medium through which Heaven can communicate to man and affect his innermost life."[28] Please synthesize this into a battle scenario.

The war that once took place in heaven is now taking place here on earth. Our mind is now the battlefield, as well as the symbol of victory that Satan seeks as his prize. Satan is doing and will continue to do everything in his powers to BREAK the "God, and the Mind-of-Man Connection."

It is because we worship God solely with our minds that the enemy Satan, who so desperately desires worship, wants to break the "God, and the Mind-of-Man Connection."

By Dr. J. Calvin Alberty

In his perverted and dark brilliance, he knows that breaking that connection will ultimately bring worship to him.

Our new mindset is all about awareness of Satan's goal. Our new mindset is to know the importance of keeping our minds secure. Our new mindset is to learn more about how to care for our brains and mind. Our new mindset is knowing that Satan's goal is to break or destroy the "GOD, AND THE MIND-OF-MAN CONNECTION" at any cost. Our new mindset is knowing that greater is He that is in us, than he that is in the world. Remember that this is only the beginning of a new mindset. There is definitely more to come.

The Two Ways and the Six Doors

There are at least two ways to access the "God, and the Mind-of-Man Connection." This connection is located in this very special place in the brain. It is where the great God of creation, redemption and salvation, has chosen to communicate with man. It is this hallowed and sacred place that Satan desires to occupy. If he cannot occupy it, then he will try to destroy it. If he cannot destroy it, then he will try to dull, distort, cloud, shroud or cloak it. If all else fails, then he will attempt to keep you ignorant of its importance, knowing that in your unawareness, a path of access to it is left unguarded. His goal is to exploit our ignorance and enter this connection through five of the six doors available to him.

Earlier, it was mentioned that there were two ways to access the "God, and the Mind-of-Man Connection." We designated one path as the path that God uses to access the "God, and the Mind-of-Man Connection." God's path is one of direct access. He can only be denied by the person refusing to give Him access. He will not force His way inside.

By Dr. J. Calvin Alberty

In an effort to clarify what is meant by this, and to place it in some understandable context, allow me to utilize the sanctuary as an illustration.

The sanctuary was a place where God met with the children of Israel. It was portable in its initial design. King Solomon would eventually erect a permanent structure. The sanctuary consisted of two compartments. The Holy Place made up about two-thirds of the sanctuary and the Most Holy Place or Holy of Holies made up about one-third of the sanctuary.

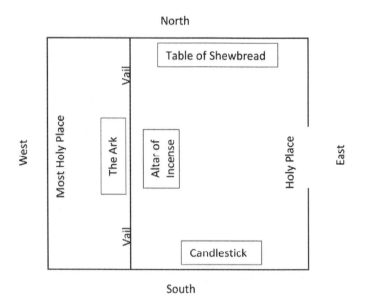

The entrance to the sanctuary was on the eastern side. There were three pieces of furniture in the Holy Place. They were the Table of Shewbread on the north wall, the candlestick, with its seven branches on the south wall, and the altar of incense that stood before the vail. The vail was the curtain that separated the Holy Place from the Most Holy Place.

There was only one piece of furniture in the Most Holy Place. It was called the Ark or the Ark of the Covenant. It was a box with a top called the Mercy Seat. Below the Mercy Seat and inside the Ark were, the Ten Commandments, a container of manna, and Aaron's rod.

This is a very simplified description of a place where almost everything was covered with gold and had a representation of our Lord. The air was fragranced with incense that represented the prayers of the believers to God. Also inside the Most Holy Place, above the Mercy Seat was the glorious Shekinah or presence of God. Every piece of furniture represented God in some special and unique way.

By Dr. J. Calvin Alberty

The purpose of the sanctuary was to be a blessing to Israel and thus to all humanity. It was here that God chose to meet with the priest, who represented the people of God (believers). In Exodus 25:8 God says, "And let them make me a sanctuary; that I may dwell among them." Do you see it here? God wants to actually be with those that He loves and those who love Him.

The people were so excited about God coming to dwell with them in a visible way until they brought offerings to Moses and the priests every morning in order to provide everything that was needed to construct the sanctuary. Notice what the book of Exodus says on this matter in Exodus 36:3 and 6, "And they received of Moses all the offering, which the children of Israel had brought for the work of the service of the sanctuary, to make it withal. And they brought yet unto him free offerings every morning. Exodus 36:6 And Moses gave commandment, and they caused it to be proclaimed throughout the camp, saying, Let neither man nor woman make any more work for the offering of the sanctuary. So the people were restrained from bringing." Isn't it amazing that the people of God gave so much and so freely until they had to be restrained or stopped from giving? They did all of this so that God could meet with them. Please remember this point for later. They sacrificed in order to have God's present with them.

When the sanctuary was finally completed, God met with man directly. It was the high priest who represented the people before God. This meeting, where the priest could come into the direct presence of God, occurred only once a year. This was known as the Day of Atonement.

Everyone in the camp of Israel from all twelve tribes saw this day as a very solemn and serious event. The priest and all of the people searched their souls for any wrongs or sins that they had committed. They confessed these sins in earnest. They believed that God would forgive them if they would confess. It would later be written in 1 John 1:9 "If we confess our sins, he is faithful and just to forgive us our sins, and to cleanse us from all unrighteousness."

By Dr. J. Calvin Alberty

This is the loving God that the people were so anxious to meet and have with them. He was their God of love as identified in Zephaniah 3:17 "The Lord thy God in the midst of thee is mighty; he will save, he will rejoice over thee with joy; he will rest in his love, he will joy over thee with singing." Yes, they sought God, and rejoiced because of His love for them. Psalm 70:4 says, "Let all those that seek thee rejoice and be glad in thee: and let such as love thy salvation say continually, Let God be magnified." The people were now following Joshua's decree of love for God. Joshua 23:11 says, "Take good heed therefore unto yourselves, that ye love the Lord your God." The children of Israel had been taught to love God. They were to see Him as life itself and the sustainer of longevity and health. Deuteronomy 30:20 conveys this when it says, "That thou mayest love the Lord thy God, and that thou mayest obey his voice, and that thou mayest cleave unto him: for he is thy life, and the length of thy days: that thou mayest dwell in the land which the Lord sware unto thy fathers, to Abraham, to Isaac, and to Jacob, to give them."

This Day of Atonement was an annual occurrence where the people with prayer and much introspection, sought to uncover every sin in their lives and confess them to God. This very special service had designed within it, a way ordained of God to remove all sin from the camp of Israel. Can you imagine what it must have been like after this solemn day had passed? The people with all sins forgiven, committed to living a life pleasing to God, must have loved just the thought of a God who wanted to restore them to wholeness, to put them at-one-ment with God.

It is in this manner that modern man must be anxious to meet with God. They must be anxious not only to meet with Him, but to have Him to not just visit, but to move in permanently into their hearts / minds.

The sanctuary of old fulfilled its purpose. All of its sacrifices and offerings all pointed to the day that Jesus would come and take all sins upon Himself and deliver man

By Dr. J. Calvin Alberty

from the bondage of sin and a fate of eternal death. John the Baptist understood this clearly when he saw Jesus approaching one day. The Bible puts it like this in John 1:2, "The next day John seeth Jesus coming unto him, and saith, Behold the Lamb of God, which taketh away the sin of the world." John knew that his purpose was now finished. It was for this purpose that John had come into the world. He was to prepare the way for Jesus. He would announce in John 1:27 that, "He it is, who coming after me is preferred before me, whose shoe's latchet I am not worthy to unloose."

He knew that Jesus was the Lamb to be slain for the sins of all. He knew that he had been called into existence for such a time, to not only prepare the way for Jesus, but to meet Him on that faith-filled day and baptize our Lord.

Read the following scriptures in Matthew 3:13-17 and visualize John's perspective of this monumental experience. "Then cometh Jesus from Galilee to Jordan unto John, to be baptized of him. 14 But John forbad him, saying, I have need to be baptized of thee, and comest thou to me? 15 And

Jesus answering said unto him, Suffer it to be so now: for thus it becometh us to fulfil all righteousness. Then he suffered him. 16 And Jesus, when he was baptized, went up straightway out of the water: and, lo, the heavens were opened unto him, and he saw the Spirit of God descending like a dove, and lighting upon him: 17 And lo a voice from heaven, saying, This is my beloved Son, in whom I am well pleased.

Can you not see this? Does this not excite everything within you? Jesus arrives from Galilee to meet John in the Jordan River. Jesus is on a divine appointment for baptism. When John sees Jesus, he is overwhelmed by his own sinful nature in the presence of what he knows to be the Son of the Living God, and he cries out, it's me Jesus. I am the one who sins need to be washed away. You are sinless, but I am a sinner in need of cleansing.

Now what John really said after forbidding Jesus was, "I have need to be baptized of thee, and comest thou to me?" Jesus knew John's apprehensive state of mind and replied,

By Dr. J. Calvin Alberty

"Suffer it to be so now: for thus it becometh us to fulfil all righteousness." Only then did John baptize Jesus. It was in obedience to his Master's request.

Jesus went from the Jordan into the wilderness, and from the wilderness of temptation, to a life of humility, sacrifice, service and love for humanity. It would be a life that would lead to the cross of Calvary, where our loving and all powerful Savior humbled Himself even to the power of death. As my favorite writers says, "Oh what matchless love."

There was something that happened on the day of Jesus' crucifixion. It happened inside of the sanctuary. The vail that separated the Holy Place from the Most Holy Place was amazingly ripped from top to bottom by unseen hands. This event is recorded in Mark 15:38 where it says, "And the veil of the temple was rent in twain from the top to the bottom." Rent in twain means torn into two pieces.

What was the meaning of this act by God? It was simple. With the death of Jesus on the cross, the sanctuary had fulfilled its earthly purpose. There would be no further need for anymore sacrifices; for now the Supreme Sacrifice had been made by our Savior. The sanctuary was built to reconnect sinful man with God by pointing to Jesus, who was and is that connection.

There would be no further need for the earthly sacrifices or the priests. Now all men could go directly to Jesus; and Jesus would intercede before the Father in heaven. To this end, 1 Timothy 2:5 says, "For there is one God, and one mediator between God and men, the man Christ Jesus." Do you realize what Jesus has done for us? Now we have open, unobstructed communication with heaven. Now God can communicate directly to our minds. In fact, it is the only means of communication that He has chosen to utilize with humanity.

I don't know about you, but I do hear His still small voice at times speaking to my mind. I, like Paul, am chief of all sinners. Yet, I have repented of my ways, and turned back to God. This wonderful God of love and forgiveness, like the father of the prodigal son in the book of Luke, He ran to meet me and made me His son again. Though so unworthy of such love, He gave it to me not because of my worthiness, but because I was so in need of it. Who would not want to love and serve a God like our God? He is always there to communicate with us? Who would not want Him to come into their heart / mind and take up permanent residence? All I have to say is PRAISE GOD! PRAISE HIS HOLY NAME!

Now that I have gotten my praise on, let's move on. Remember that we were using the sanctuary to explain one of the two ways mentioned to access the "God, and the Mind-of-Man Connection." We were specifically talking about the path that God uses to access this "God, and the Mind-of-Man Connection." We said that God's path is one of direct access.

It is direct access just as it was when God met with the representative of humanity in the Most Holy place. Just as He said In Exodus 25:8, "And let them make me a sanctuary; that I may dwell among them." This is still God's desire to dwell in our body temple in our Most Holy Place. It is the Most Holy Place in the sense that it is where God meets directly with us. We should be just like those who gave to build the sanctuary. We should give of ourselves sacrificially so that we can meet with God.

In essence we should sacrifice our time, appetites, ways, attitudes, bad habits, treasure, will, the things of this world and all to Christ. Everything about us should be defined in seeking first the Kingdom of God and the desire to have Him to communicate with and guide our every decision.

God has direct access to our minds, yet He will never force His will upon us. He will never dwell or enter our minds without our consent. He wants to be there only if we love Him and want Him there.

Then there is the enemy of every earthly soul; the ever stalking dark antagonist on this stage called life. He is Satan. He cannot directly access our minds. He cannot force his way in and exert his will without us first giving our consent.

By Dr. J. Calvin Alberty

So how does Satan indirectly gain access to our minds? The answer is through the senses of the body.

"The BODY is a MOST IMPORTANT medium through which the mind and the soul are DEVELOPED for the up-building of character." [29] So what is this really saying? It is saying that the mind is developed through the body for building character. It is saying that what we do to and with our bodies has an intimate relationship to the development or decline of our minds and character. The mind-body connection is really an inextricable connection. The mind and body work as one. Do you hear what is being said? They work as one.

"Hence it is that the adversary of souls directs his temptations to the enfeebling and degrading of the physical powers . . ." (BODY). "His success here" (in the body) "often means the surrender of the WHOLE being to evil."[30]

This means that Satan knows that he cannot directly access the "God, and the Mind-of-Man Connection." He is powerless on this point. However, notice what is being said.

Satan directs his efforts toward the body, because he knows that if he successfully overcomes the person on this point, then that would mean, "the surrender of the whole being to evil."

Get it? If he gets the body, the whole man or woman will succumb or surrender to evil. In essence, to Satan, getting the body is getting the mind. He sees no distinction. Satan also knows the nature of the connection of the body and mind. He is very aware of how effective his tactics have worked with billions of lost souls that he has sent to Christless graves. He sent them there throughout the ages by way of their bodies of flesh.

Satan, who is full of wisdom, not only understands this flesh and mind connection very well. He also understands the intimate connections of the mind of man with God. He full well understands that to control the body is to control the mind, and to control the mind is to control the man, and to control the man is to have him to reject God. It is for this reason that Satan has launched an all-out attack against the body and mind of man. Our focus for now is on the body.

So, how does Satan get control over the body of man? Here's the answer. God has direct access to the mind (one door), while Satan has direct access to the body. His avenues to the body is through the five senses (five doors). These are the six doors. God uses one, while Satan uses five. God has a way (direct access to the mind), while Satan has a way (direct access to the body). Thus the title of this chapter, "The Two Ways and the Six Doors."

Guard Well the Avenues of the Soul

Getting to the mind, through the senses, is extremely important to Satan. He knows that he has no other way. He also knows that to do so will give him control of everything. By so doing, he knows that he will successfully lead man to a fate most sorry. This is why Paul says in 1 Corinthians 9:27, "But I keep under my body, and bring it into subjection … (KJV). In the International Standard Version 1 Corinthians 9:27 reads like this, "No, I keep on disciplining my body, making it serve me."

So if we do not bring our bodies under subjection to serve us to the glory of God; then we can be certain that our bodies will surely bring us into subjection to serve it. Then our body becomes our god. Understand, that when the body becomes our god, then all of the senses of the body become open doors for Satan to gain access to our minds and the "God, and the Mind-of-Man Connection."

Imagine, if you will, Satan going from door to door of your senses LOOKING for a way in. The reason that he is looking for a way in is because he does not have the power to force his way in. If he could he would, but he cannot do so. "The tempter can never compel us to do evil. He cannot control our minds unless they are yielded to his control."[31]

Satan can never compel or force us to sin. He cannot compel us to let him into the throne-room of our mind. Jesus doesn't compel us and praise God, He does not allow our adversary to do it. Jesus says in Revelation 3:20, "Behold, I stand at the door, and knock: if any man hears my voice, and opens the door, I will come in to him, and will sup with him, and he with me." Notice that Jesus stands at the door and knocks. He does not have a battering-ram. Instead He stands and waits patiently for each of us to invite Him in.

Satan must stand at the doors to our senses until he is allowed in; and only we can do that. We must be incredibly careful because, "Every sinful desire we cherish affords him a foothold. Every point in which we fail of meeting the divine standard, is an OPEN DOOR by which he can enter to tempt and destroy us.[32] This is a Biblical echo of what John 10:10

says, "The thief cometh not, but for to steal, and to kill, and to destroy." Be ever mindful that since his fall this has always been Satan's goal. He will do everything and anything in his power to kill and destroy those for whom Jesus died.

Safety is in obedience to God's word. Safety is in the grace and mercy of Jesus. However, the Bible says in, Matthew 4:7, Jesus said unto him, "It is written again, "Thou shalt not tempt the Lord thy God." So we must not be presumptive in our behaviors or our thoughts. We must not lean on our own understanding. Again, I repeat, our safety is in loving Jesus. And He said in John 14:15. "If ye love me, keep my commandments."

The safety is in the love of, and the obedience to God. This type of obedience must come, and can only come as a result of loving God and not trying to earn or merit His grace, which is so freely given. Satan sees the Christian who obeys God out of love as having an impenetrable mind. He knows that he cannot force his way into their mind. However, he does not stop making every effort. 1 Peter 5:8 warns us to

By Dr. J. Calvin Alberty

"Be sober, be vigilant; because your adversary the devil, as a roaring lion, walketh about, seeking whom he may devour." Do you see what is being said here? He goes about as a roaring lion attacking the senses, constantly looking for ways through doors that should be locked. He is constantly checking every door to our senses, so that he can seize upon any opportunity presenting itself to destroy us by destroying the "God, and the Mind-of-Man Connection."

It is for this reason that we are admonished to be careful. "You will have to become a faithful sentinel over your eyes, ears, and all of your senses if YOU would control your mind and prevent vain and corrupt thoughts from staining your soul."[33]

This war against the flesh is no joke. In fact, it is overwhelming for the flesh, which is our body and our senses. It is overwhelming because the flesh is weak! Matthew 26:41 calls us to "Watch and pray, that ye enter not into temptation: the spirit indeed is willing, but the flesh is weak."

The flesh will lose every time if left to stand in the battle alone. However, if we allow Jesus to occupy the throne-room of our minds, then we will discover like the Bible says in 2 Chronicles 20:15, ". . . Thus saith the Lord unto you, Be not afraid nor dismayed by reason of this great multitude; for the battle is not yours, but God's." 2 Chronicles 20:17 adds to this, ". . . fear not, nor be dismayed; tomorrow go out against them: for the Lord will be with you."

This is the good news. We are not alone in the battle for our minds. Zechariah 4:6 reminds us that this battle is, ". . . Not by might, nor by power, but by my spirit, saith the Lord of hosts." We cannot lose in our warfare over the flesh if we do not purposely block God out of our lives, while diligently guarding the senses. So why do we not guard the senses the way that we should in the first place? Maybe it is because most of us do not know just how important it is to do so.

Even though we have heard the warnings in the Bible, many still do not grasp the gravity of this issue. Even though

By Dr. J. Calvin Alberty

2Corinthians 3:18 says, "But we all, with open face beholding as in a glass the glory of the Lord, are changed into the same image from glory to glory, even as by the Spirit of the Lord." It is saying that we are changed into what we behold or look at or ponder on. It says, in short, that by beholding we become changed.

So how then do we behold? Simply put, the five senses. Consider the words of Psalm 101:3, "I will set no wicked thing before mine eyes." God is saying here, guard well the avenues to the mind. All of these warnings have done little to abate Satan victories. Why do we continue to expose our senses to any and every vile creation of the enemy? Even though Habakkuk 1:13 says, "Your eyes are too pure to gaze upon evil; and you cannot tolerate wickedness."

Pure eyes are the eyes of the godly, who love Jesus. The way that many of us use television is like taking a train headed for destruction, while we are enamored, charmed and captivated by the scenes passing by outside the windows of the train. So why do we do this? Why do we sit there and allow television to pump so much garbage into our minds? Why do we listen to any and every kind of vile song to our own destruction? Because either we do not know the foolishness or deadliness of our behaviors, or we are dull of mind and just do not take God seriously!

Notice in the following scripture that Isaiah also speaks of guarding the avenues to the soul. Isaiah 33:15 says, "The one who walks righteously and has spoken sincere words, who rejects gain from extortion and waves his hand, rejecting bribes, **who blocks his ears** from hearing plots of murder and **shuts his eyes against seeing evil."** Isaiah is speaking here about guarding well the avenues to the mind.

Joe Crews wrote a wonderful book entitled "Enemy at the Gate." Someone commented on the book saying, "In a culture that constantly assaults our senses with every kind of soul-destroying temptation, this amazing book will give you the keys and the inspiration to stay pure for God."

So we are warned by God, Ellen White, Joe Crews, and the Bible to guard well the avenues of the soul, which are the senses. Ellen White says, "All should guard the senses, lest Satan gain victory over them; for these are the avenues of the soul."[34] However, many will not heed these warnings about guarding the senses. Why? I think the answer lies in the possibility that whereas Satan was once at the gate as warned by Joe Crews, I believe that the enemy is now inside many gates.

It is easy to conceive that this is the case because "Satan and his angels are busy creating a PARALYZED condition of the senses so that cautions, warnings, and reproofs shall not be heard; or, if heard, that they shall not take effect upon the heart and reform the life."[35]

This mental paralysis leads to confusion! "Satan's Strategy Is to Confuse the Senses—Satan's work is to lead men to ignore God, to so engross and absorb the mind that God will not be in their thoughts. The education they have received has been of a character to CONFUSE the mind and eclipse the true light."[36] Confuse the mind? Where does this confusion come from? 1 Corinthians 14:33 gives the answer,

"For God is not the author of confusion. . ." If God is not the author of confusion, then who is this author? It is Satan. This confusion comes as a result of weak and enfeebled minds that Satan has accessed via the senses and is now working to completely destroy. This continues to occur because many still do not take it seriously, when they are warned to **GUARD WELL THE AVENUES OF THE SOUL!**

By Dr. J. Calvin Alberty

Weak and Enfeebled Minds (Mind Seduction)

Anything that lessens physical strength (lack of exercise, lack of sleep, eating the wrong or too much food) enfeebles the mind and makes it less capable of discriminating between right and wrong.[37] This is the very definition of CONFUSION. Please note that she highlights three mind enfeeblers here in this one paragraph. They are lack of exercise, lack of sleep, and eating the wrong or too much food. It is astounding how these three behaviors tie together so seamlessly. Let's look at how they interact.

If you stay up late at night, you will eat. Then you will eat some more. After eating late at night, your sleep is disturbed and your stomach works all night long, so that you wake up tired in the morning. Now you are too tired to exercise, so you lie around looking at television or being involved in some other inactivity. You nap or nod during the day, so you stay in this fatigued state of mind. It is now time to go to bed, but you are not really sleepy. You are not sleepy because you napped and nodded throughout the day, so you stay up and start the whole cycle over again. You continue in this behavior until a pattern develops (of which we will speak about later). These patterns develop into strong habits. The habits become more like reflexes. This means that they become like automatic or reflexive responses that require very little thought. "It is now widely accepted that instrumental actions can be either goal-directed or habitual; whereas the former are rapidly acquired and regulated by their outcome, the latter are reflexive, elicited by antecedent stimuli rather than their consequences."[38]

Do you grasp what this is saying? In a nutshell it is saying that our behaviors can be habitual and reflexive. Another word for reflexive is automatic. Our behavior therefore can become automatic responses, regardless of their consequences. This is the case because the behaviors are driven and guided by automatic responses to our environment. B. F. Skinner termed this as "Operant Conditioning." This is when the environment elicit automatic responses from us, because it has reinforced those responses in the past via our interactions with said environment.

In its simplest form, it means that we stop thinking and start reacting. Satan loves this type of behavior, because now he can plot and plan to seduce our senses without ever going directly through our mind. He exploits the sensory responses by reinforcing them with pleasure. The truth is, what feels good we are likely to repeat. Perhaps this is a good place to take a moment to look back at two points that we mentioned earlier. We stated that:

1. Satan enters the mind through our five senses by way of our physical bodies.

2. We also stated that we will have to become faithful sentinels over our eyes, ears, and all of our senses if we would be in control of our mind.[39]

Allow me to assert that you cannot be a faithful sentinel if you are confused, mentally debilitated, mentally enfeebled, a mental wreck, or if your mind is so weak and enfeebled that you are absent minded and you are constantly forgetting

By Dr. J. Calvin Alberty

things, especially the importance of being a faithful sentinel. I am mentioning this for a reason. You will find out in a moment why this point is being made. But in the meanwhile, let me ask this question. Which of the five senses do you think is the greatest cause of physical and mental debility? It is the sense of taste, which we will now delve into.

Appetite

Notice what Ellen White says on this subject. "Appetite is the greatest cause of physical and mental debility and lies at the foundation of the feebleness which is apparent everywhere."[40] This really opened my eyes. This statement alone, succinctly encapsulates the greatest cause of feebleness of the brain. It is the indulgence of appetite.

"Through appetite Satan controls the mind and the whole being. Thousands who might have lived have passed into the grave as physical, mental, and moral wrecks, because they sacrificed. . ."[41] This quote is being cut off here to address the phrase "because they sacrificed."

Isn't a sacrifice something that was done to God's glory and for man's good before the crucifixion of Christ? Remember this as you continue to read the entire statement (which follows) with the understanding that we sacrifice to GOD! "Through appetite Satan controls the mind and the whole being. Thousands who might have lived have passed into the grave as physical, mental, and moral wrecks, because they sacrificed ALL their powers to the indulgence of appetite."[42] Wow! All I can say is wow. Listen.

1. Satan uses appetite to control the mind.

2. The mind controls the whole being.

3. The person sacrifices all of their powers to appetite.

4. Remember that we make sacrifices to God

5. So we are not just sacrificing our powers to our appetite, but to our god "the appetite."

6. So in essence, Satan gets us to replace the true God, with the god called "appetite."

7. And all of our powers are sacrificed to the indulgence of the "appetite god."

Before we move on to the next chapter, the question that must now be answered is who is this appetite god? Does he work alone or in conjunction with other gods? I think that you will find that the answer to this will be very interesting, and maybe even surprising.

Our Belly as God

What did we mean by statement number seven when we stated, "And all of our powers are sacrificed to the indulgence of the "appetite god?" This means that to the indulgence of appetite, we have sacrificed our physical powers, our mental powers, our spiritual powers, our emotional powers and so-forth. They were all, every one of them, sacrificed to the indulgence of appetite! If we look carefully at the altar of our sacrifice, we will see something languishing there. It will be our "will." It will be there because every time we surrender in any way to Satan's urges, our will to resist becomes weakened.

Now here it is in A, B, C form.

A. Since sacrifices are to be made to God.

B. And we are sacrificing ALL of our powers to our appetite

C. Then our bellies must be our gods.

The Bible echoes this by saying in, Philippians 3:18-20 "For many walk, of whom I have told you often, and now tell you even weeping, that they are the enemies of the cross of Christ: 19 Whose end is destruction, whose God is their belly. . ." With this in mind, now let me rephrase an earlier quote from Ellen White. Through appetite Satan enslaves our mind and our entire being. Like thousands of others we will pass into early graves as physical, mental, and moral wrecks, because we continue to sacrifice ALL of our powers on the altar of indulgence to appetite, who is our God, THE BELLY.

The belly god often calls for us to be gourmands, which are in fact gluttons. Ellen White addressed such a person as this by writing, "You are a gourmand when at the table. This is one great cause of your forgetfulness and loss of memory."[43] Now this is interesting, especially as we age. I once wondered how much stuff I was forgetting as a result of aging over the life span. Now I am concern about how much is being forgotten because of how I use my knife, fork and spoon, and what I put on them and place in my body?

Does "our" god the appetite or belly work alone? I am speaking here "inclusively," saying "our" not because appetite is our god, but as a warning that we do not allow him to become our god, unless the same fate that awaits other idolaters, will also befall us. Now to answer the question. No, the appetite god does not work alone. I will not go into a lot of detail here, but will instead try to answer this with an illustration that will hopefully make it very clear.

The nostril god smells a wonderful odor representing your favorite food. The eye god then gazes upon it and agrees with the nostril god that this is something that should be sought after as a meal. The ear god hears others talking about how good it tastes. The body god then coordinate efforts with the hands to put some of what we see, smell, and hear others speaking about, on our plate to be eaten. The touch god loves the way it feels against the palate and side of the mouth. It loves the way it feels going down the esophagus as we are swallowing it. Finally the taste god is overwhelmed by how good it taste. All gods agree that they want to do this again. Throw temperance out of the window they say. They agree that when the next opportunity comes, they will not even have to think about it. They will just eat it until they can eat no more. Then all five of these gods turn toward the belly god and bow down to worship him. The belly god then looks toward the throne room of the mind and yells out, "It won't be long now."

He says this knowing that bit-by-bit and step-by-step, he is taking control of the "God, and the Mind-of-Man Connection." One fork-full at a time, one heaping spoon after another, one slice at a time, he is carving out his territory in mind where he will eventually reign supreme over the "God, and the Mind-of-Man Connection."

The Starved and Dizzy Brain

How can the stomach or belly become our god? Really, how can this be, especially when our brain is where our intelligence resides? After all, isn't the brain where we reason, feel, think, imagine, work difficult puzzles, and make choices? How can this happen? Is the brain sleeping on the job? Well after you read the following maybe you will come to the same conclusion this author has reached.

Think about the glutton that we spoke about earlier. Let's focus on him. He will be our focal point because his behavior will give us insight into the answers we are seeking. Here's a clue in the form of a question. What activity of the body requires the most energy to accomplish?

Sara Tomm cites the October 2004 issue of the "Journal of the American College of Nutrition" where an article was published stating that "animal protein takes longer to digest than carbohydrates or fat, and uses 20 to 35 percent of calories (energy) to complete the digestive process." [44]

By Dr. J. Calvin Alberty

We find the following information in "The American Journal of Clinical Nutrition," which states that the energy expenditure for digestion was highest for protein based meals. On average, it was 17% higher after the protein meal and 27% higher after the alcohol meal.[45]

As you can see, with 17 to 35 percent of the body's energy going to the stomach for digestion and metabolism, not to mention all of the other bodily functions that require energy, the poor brain is being starved. In essence, most of the vital energies of the blood are spent in the stomach aiding in digestion, while the brain is crying for support.

"The digestive organs, like a mill which is continually kept running, become enfeebled, vital force is called from the brain to aid the stomach in its overwork, and thus the mental powers are weakened…"[46] This is understandable when you consider the unrelenting effort by the stomach to take care of someone who eats throughout the day, snacking, eating meals, more snacking, eating more meals, etc. I am sure that you get the picture. If not, then consider this little illustration. I come to you and I ask you to do stomach crunches or pull-ups. You agree. I then ask you to do this continually without stopping until I tell you. So you get started and continue to do so while waiting on me to ask you to stop, which I never do. How long can you last? The length of time really does not matter. What does matter is the fact that you will at some point in time eventually quit as a result of muscle fatigue.

With this in mind, think of the poor stomach being bathed in hydrochloric acid while having to continually digest food. It's waiting for you to stop eating, but the food keeps coming. It has no choice, it must keep working as long as food is in need of digestion.

The poor stomach notices that you are eating the foods that require the most energy to break down. It is so very exhausted, but still continues to work. It is out of energy, so it now takes the energy from anywhere in the body that it can. The brain is also a high energy user. They both cannot continue to use the limited energy, one must yield. The one that will always eventually yield is the brain, because the stomach has no choice. IT MUST WORK. It must work because someone will not give it a break. And thus "the mental powers are weakened."

The weakening of the mental powers are never good. This is the case because the brain controls everything in the body. The body and brain have an intimate and reciprocal relationship between them. "The condition of the mind affects the health to a far greater degree than many realize."[47]

The Tremendous Power of the Mind

The human mind is something very special in its abilities to create. The very nature of God is one of being a Creator, and we were made in His image. To get a glimpse into the depth of the mind's powers, just contemplate on these two Bible verses. Genesis 11:6 "And the Lord said, Behold, the people is one, and they have all one language; and this they begin to do: and now nothing will be restrained from them, which they have imagined to do."

This first text really requires focused thought. Just think of the condition of the hearts or minds of these people when God spoke this statement. We find the condition of their hearts in Genesis 6:5. "And God saw that the wickedness of man was great in the earth, and that every imagination of the thoughts of his heart was only evil continually."

Here is the main point that these two texts bring together. These people were extremely bad people. God says that their thoughts were not only evil, but they were evil continually. Yet, as evil as they were, God said that they could do anything that they put their minds to. Nothing would be restrained from them. This says that the mind has tremendous power. These words actually boggle the mind. I believe that God made this declaration so that we could get a sense of the power that He has invested in the human mind. Imagine, even though these people were doing everything in their power to go against God, and even though they were extremely evil, vile and perverse, still, their minds could do anything that they could imagine. It has to make you ask another question like, what kind of mind did God give to man; and how amazing was this mind before almost 6000 years of sin deleteriously affected it?

Here's the other verse that tells us about the mind. It is found in Proverbs 23:7, "For as he thinketh in his heart, so is he." Can you grab hold of the enormity of this Bible verse? It is saying whatever we think, or whatever we believe, we have the power to become that or to do that. This is the awesome potential for greatness that God has placed within the mind of each and every one of us. We saw this demonstrated in the Bible, when in Israel, a certain leader's daughter was dead and the leader received the heart breaking announcement in the presence of Jesus. As the announcement is made by others, Jesus calls out to the leader. His name is Jairus. Jesus says these two power filled words, "Only believe."

I get goose bumps just thinking about it. My pulse races and I breathe deeply and rapidly when I think about how exciting it must have been to stand in the presence of such love and power as our Savior possesses. In saying, ONLY BELIEVE," Jesus was declaring the power of faith, which is a belief in God's ability to do anything for His children. He was also declaring the power of our minds, when they are connected with Him.

One last thought on this amazing power of the mind. Think about its power as you read this next text. Proverbs 18:21 says, "Death and life are in the power of the tongue..." Whoa! Do you mean we have the ability to speak life into a dead situation? Yes, but just like Jesus said to Jairus, all we have to do is, "ONLY BELIEVE."

I also see this in Aaron's rod. Though it was a stick that was formerly a branch cut from a tree, it budded and bloomed. Listen to the book of Hebrews in Hebrews 9:4, "Which had the golden censer, and the ark of the covenant overlaid round about with gold, wherein was the golden pot that had manna, and **Aaron's rod that budded**, and the tables of the covenant." This stick was supposed to be dead. It had been separated or cut from the tree. Yet it budded. IT SHOULD HAVE BEEN DEAD! This is representative of the unlimited power of God to speak life into our dead situations. These are situations like the leader's dead daughter. We must be so careful with our tongue and what we say. If we ONLY BELIEVE, and speak those things that are not, as though they were, then we will begin to comprehend the power that God has placed in the human mind.

We must also understand that the mind and the body are connected as one. That is why, whatever we think we are, then we are; or it is what we are becoming. Henry Ford said, "If you think you can or can't, you're right." Don't you see it? Our destiny is in our thinking, because our thinking makes us who we are and takes us where we are going!

My favorite author writes, "Many of the diseases from which men suffer are the result of mental depression, grief, anxiety, discontent, remorse, guilt, distrust, all tend to break down the life forces and to invite decay and death."[48] Do you get what she is saying? Many of our diseases come from the mind. She clarifies this further when she writes, "Disease is sometimes produced, and is often greatly aggravated, by the imagination (of the mind). Many are lifelong invalids who might be well if they only thought so."[49] OH MY GOODNESS! Disease is sometimes the result of our imagination, and many might be well if they ONLY THOUGHT so? This is incredible, but it is definitely the truth!

I have two quick examples. They are placebos and witch doctors. Placebo therapy has proven effective in many cases. The person may be hypochondriacal (only think they

By Dr. J. Calvin Alberty

are sick). They think they are ill, so they are ill. They present all of the symptoms of a person with the actual sickness that they express having. The doctor then prescribes some harmless inert pills (placebos). The patient takes the pills and professes shortly afterward that they are doing fine. Yes, they are doing fine because they THINK the placebos are medicines with active ingredients that cured them. Just like they thought they were sick, now they think they are well, so they are well. It was all about their thinking.

The witch doctor on the other hand has no powers at all. Well let me put it like this. The witch doctor has powers, because the people within his culture think he does. It is their thinking that gives him power over them. Many would never be subject to his influence if they only thought differently. What are you thinking about your situations? Remember, the mind has tremendous power. So, I ask again, what are you thinking about your situation? Are you putting the mind's tremendous powers to work for you or against you?

The Reciprocal Nature of the Mind and Body

Never forget what was said earlier. The mind and the body function as one. As much as we would like to see them as separate entities, they are not. Listen. You are you. Everything about you makes you who you are, YOU. If we step back and look at it like a child, it isn't complicated. When I speak to you, I am not speaking to your big toe, your foot, your leg, or your body. I am not speaking to your mind, emotions, or anything other than the whole person. I AM SPEAKING TO YOU. Like I said, it isn't complicated, the mind and the body are inextricably one.

We just witnessed in the previous chapter the command or power that the mind has over the body, so let's now look at the influence that the body has on the mind. The purpose here is to see that this is a two way street, because the two are one. Not only does the mind affects the body, but the body also affects the mind.

Ellen White writes under the title of "Mental Effort Affected by Physical Vigor" "We should seek to preserve the full vigor of all our powers for the accomplishment of the work before us. Whatever detracts from physical vigor weakens mental effort. Hence, every practice unfavorable to the health of the body should be resolutely shunned."[50]

There it is, a very simple statement filled with atomic power. "Whatever detracts from physical vigor weakens mental effort." So, whatever affects the body, also affects the mind. This is the reciprocal nature of the mind and body.

With this knowledge, we must begin the formation of a new mindset. It is a mindset that is formed with the understanding that:

1. WHAT you put into your body impacts your mind.

2. WHAT you eat contributes to making you who you are as well as who you are now becoming.

3. Mental health is physical health and physical health is mental health

4. WHEN you feed the mind you feed the body and when you feed the body you feed the mind.

5. WHEN you injure the mind you injure the body and when you injure the body you injure the mind.

I want to repeat something here before closing this chapter. "The tempter can never compel us to do evil. He cannot control minds unless they are yielded to his control."[51] In light of this statement, I believe that God warns us all, that we must be very careful in knowingly going against His health principles.

Remember, it is through appetite that Satan most effectively controls the mind. So we must understand that if we are not careful, we could very well, with our forks, spoons and knives, be unwittingly yielding our minds to Satan.

When people say that diet has nothing to do with our salvation, they are either naïve, ignorant, or they are untruthful. I mean, if you really think about it, isn't that exactly what happened to Adam and Eve? Did they not yield their minds to Satan at the point of appetite by knowingly disobeying God? Hence, man fell and his fall instituted the need for the plan of salvation (as they say) in the first place?

By Dr. J. Calvin Alberty

Really Beginning A New Mindset

Let's look what beginning a new mindset really means. It means:

1. You know that your mind is the ONLY point that God communicates with you.

2. You know that your mind worships God.

3. You know that the devil knows this too.

4. You know that Satan is doing everything that he can to destroy the "GOD, AND THE MIND-OF-MAN CONNECTION."

5. You know that Satan can only access your mind through the senses (the body).

6. You know therefore that you must guard well the avenues of the mind.

7. You know that the body and mind is one and that what you feed the body, you feed to strengthen or enfeeble BOTH the mind and the body.

8. You know that appetite is Satan's major highway to the mind.

9. You know that we either serve God or our flesh

10. You know that what we eat affects our mind, our body and our choices relative to salvation.

11. You know that if you knowingly eat habitually wrong, then your belly is your god, which by default will make Satan your god.

12. You know that unless God sits on the throne of your mind, your appetite will dull your mind, paralyze your senses, debilitate your mind and body, and allow Satan to sit on the throne of your mind as god.

13. You've got to know, that this ultimately connects appetite with salvation, because you cannot hear God if your mind will not allow Him to communicate with you. You cannot worship God sincerely when the mind is debilitated; and it is the mind that we worship God with. And this condition will only worsen, because the reward pathways and neural connections in the pleasure region of your brain have made you a food junkie, just as hooked on food as an addict on cocaine or alcohol.

Allow me to share this data before moving on to point number fourteen. "Finally, various types of studies indicate an overlap between mechanisms mediating drug reward and palatable food reward. Preference or consumption of sweet substances often parallels the self-administration of several drugs of abuse, and under certain conditions, the termination of intermittent access to sweet substances produces symptoms that resemble those observed during opiate withdrawal."[52] Gosnell, B. A., & Levine, A. S. (2009). I know that you hear what this is saying. It states that the mechanisms that reward drug users are the same as those that reward the consumption of palatable food.

It further states that individuals who have a preference for sweets are similar to those individuals who self-administers drugs of abuse. It finally says that under certain conditions, cutting off a person's access to sweets produces symptoms that are similar to those observed in people going through opiate withdrawal. Now can you understand why I made the statement earlier that certain foods, more than others, stimulate the pleasure region of your brain and have made you as much of a food junkie, as an addict who is hooked on cocaine or alcohol.

14. We must realize that the things that we place in our mouths have a direct effect on the only thing that you and I truly have as human beings. And that is . . . **THE GOD GIVEN POWER OF CHOICE!**

THE GOD GIVEN POWER OF CHOICE!

Please notice that I did not just say the power of choice. Instead, I said the "God given" power of choice. Choice is like grace. It was never something that we earned. It was not something that we deserved. It was a reflection of God's love for us. He gave it to us.

How we utilize this amazing power is also an expression of who we have become and who we are becoming. Every choice that we make further clarifies **who** we really are; **whose** we really are; and **where** we plan on going. Simply put, choices are destinations. In fact, we should never make a choice without thinking, "Will this move me closer to Jesus, or away from Him. Will this move me toward my desired destination (heaven) or away from it? Will this lift Jesus up or lift up the enemy of souls?" Remember this, you should know that every choice has a direction and a destiny, even if you are not aware of what they are.

Listen, this power of choice is one of the most awe inspiring gifts ever given by God! It was man's mis-utilization of this power that placed Jesus (because of His love) on the cross. How powerful is that?! Anything that powerful, we as humans could never earn or merit. If man had earned it, he would have the right to use it in any manner that he wanted to. That is why we must know that it is a God-given gift.

Notice this, "God has given us the power of choice; it is ours to exercise."[53] Notice that Ellen White says that it was given to us to exercise. Let me ask you, have you ever heard of a steward? Have you ever heard of stewardship? Being a steward who practices good stewardship, means that you have in your care something that has been given to you by someone else. Whatever that "something" is, you are to manage it in the best interest of the person who gave it to you and entrusted you with it.

When the person returns, you will have to give them an account of how you managed their property or whatever it was that they placed in your care. This would include our body, our mind, our choices, etc.

To this author, this is exactly the case with the power of choice. We will have to give an account of how we used this extremely exceptional gift or power. The Lord has a question for us all. "How have you been using My gift, the power of choice, given to you to be my steward over?" Do you think for one second, that our incredible and awesome God, who counts the very hairs on our heads (Matthew 10:30) is indifferent as to how we use the power of choice?

Do you think that our great God, who says that not one idle word escapes Him (Matthew 12:36) "But I say unto you, That every idle word that men shall speak, they shall give account thereof in the day of judgment." Do you really believe that He will not be monitoring how we use something as compelling a gift as the "POWER OF CHOICE"?

By Dr. J. Calvin Alberty

The Subconscious / Unconscious Mind

The debate of the term subconscious as oppose to the unconscious can be an issue with some people, so let me clarify the usage that I have chosen for this book. Let me begin by sharing parts of an article from the Harvard Health Blog. The article is entitled *Unconscious or Subconscious?* It is written by Michael Craig Miller, M.D., Senior Editor, Mental Health Publishing for Harvard Health Publication. He writes, "As for the term "subconscious," Freud used it interchangeably with "unconscious" at the outset." He continues, "The words are similarly close but not identical in German (subconscious is das Unterbewusste; unconscious is das Unbewusste). But he eventually stuck with the latter term to avoid confusion."[54]

So we see that Freud eventually stuck with the term "unconscious." However, Doctor Miller does go on to assert that generally in the professional realm the term unconscious is used. He adds, "Although the word subconscious continues to appear in the lay literature."[55]

By Dr. J. Calvin Alberty

Though this book is written for lay people relative to psychology, I will make use of the professional terminology of "unconscious." I wish that when it came to the use of "unconscious" or "subconscious" this was the only relative issue. However, there are others who ascribe to the belief that "The mind should be divided into three systems: the conscious mind, the subconscious mind, and the unconscious mind"[56] Corsini, R. J., & Wedding, D. (2011). Hmmm, that's another story altogether. So let's move forward.

Do We Have Control or Not?

Listen to an interesting quote by Ellen White, "God has given us the power of CHOICE; it is ours to exercise. We cannot change our hearts, we cannot control our thoughts, our impulses, our affections. We cannot make ourselves pure, fit for God's service. But we can CHOOSE to serve God ...[57]

This is a powerful statement. I mean, did God not give us the power of choice? So what is specifically meant by "We cannot change our hearts (mind), we cannot control our thoughts, our impulses, our affections?" How can this statement be correct if we are understood to be God-given possessors of the "Power of Choice?" Let me put it in the vernacular of what the kids on the corner might say, "I'm just saying."

This is a significant statement. We are compelled to investigate it deeper. So, why can't we change our hearts (minds), thoughts and impulses? We do have the power of choice, do we not? Well, do we? Certainly we do. So let's delve deeper into this interesting and captivating subject of the unconscious mind.

The Bible actually speaks about this heart or mind that we cannot change in no uncertain terms. It says in Jeremiah 17:9 "The HEART is deceitful above all things, and desperately wicked: WHO CAN KNOW IT?" WHO CAN KNOW IT? WHO CAN KNOW IT? This is a question worth asking over and over again. Here's what I gather from it.

I believe that it says "who can know it," because the mind has a deep hidden portion that is unknown. This area is not so much anatomical as it is functional. It is so named relative to our ability, or should I say our inability to access it. It is called the "unconscious" because we do not have the cognitive ability to pull that file drawer open and open a folder and peruse its content. In this analogy, see the file cabinet as locked without a readily accessible key to open it. However, there is a key. It is a key whose location we do not know. This key lies in the hand of two characters that we will call "life events" and "life circumstances." They show up when they want to, not on demand. They can show up at any time or never show up at all.

When they do show up, we are not allowed to view the entire content of the file cabinet; not even a whole drawer; and needless to say, not even a complete file-folder. These two characters only give us access to a part of a miniscule portion of the folder. It is that portion that is relevant to our immediate or recent experiences coloring that moment.

It may give access to repressed memories, skewed schemas, beliefs, previous experiences, and other unconscious elements that are continuously and unknowingly influencing our thoughts. These thoughts influence our behaviors and the choices we make. In other words, these thoughts influence our every moment while we live on this earth. Deeper still, these thoughts can control us in such a manner as to even shape our eternal destiny.

Now back to Jeremiah 17:9 which says, "The heart is deceitful above all things, and desperately wicked: who can know it?" Let's make sure we are standing on the same

By Dr. J. Calvin Alberty

ground in regards to the word "heart." I know that this word "heart" means the "mind." I just want to make sure that you also know this. Of course it has other meanings, but let's look at this particular meaning for now.

Let's look at this word used for "heart" in other biblical scriptures. However, let me set the stage by asking, what do we think or imagine with; our brain or our heart? Now here's the Bible verse. Acts 8:22 says, "Repent therefore of this thy wickedness, and pray God, if perhaps the THOUGHT OF THINE HEART may be forgiven thee." Again, what do we think and have thoughts with"? It is our brain and not our heart.

Let's check out another Bible verse. Genesis 6:5 says, "And GOD saw that the wickedness of man was great in the earth, and that every imagination of the thoughts of his heart was only evil continually." You have to admit that we imagine and think with our brain/mind and not our heart. However, if you need more information in order to settle this issue, then I will give you more.

Another way to know that "heart" means "mind" in many places in the Bible is to look it up in the original Hebrew language. The Hebrew word for heart is leb, בָּ‏ב‏ֵל (Strong's reference # H3824). It is pronounced as (LAVE). It means among other things: conscience, mind, knowledge, thinking, reflection, memory, and interestingly enough, it is also referred to as the seat of appetites.[58] Hopefully, that is enough to make sure that we are all standing on level ground in understanding that often in the Bible, the word heart refers to the human mind.

Now back to our question, what is meant by "We cannot change our hearts (mind), we cannot control our thoughts, our impulses, our affections?" To answer this question, I must first ask, did you know that most of the thoughts that steer the human mind are at the subconscious level?

I am referring to the 35,000 to 49,000 negative thoughts that we are estimated to have each day. One of the issues that give rise to all of these negative thoughts is that many of us have too much junk stuffed in our trunks at the

By Dr. J. Calvin Alberty

unconscious level. Here' a poem that I wrote some years ago to address this point. It is entitled, "I Lug the Suitcase."

I LUG THE SUITCASE

There's too much stuff in our suitcases,

Holding us down and keeping us back,

Deuces without any kings and no aces,

Making us walk on a circular track.

Locking us in and locking us out,

Breaking our spirits tearing us down

When we could win, making us doubt,

When we could smile, making us frown.

Too much junk stuffed in our trunk,

Tired and discouraged we tug and we toil.

We sleep to escape it, like one who is drunk.

The guilt and the pain that is wound like a coil,

Ready to spring, to spin and unwind

But locking it tight I keep everything in.

But somehow it finds me, my past from behind

The hurt others caused and my own haunting sins.

Like a bag lady I still lug around,

Yesterday's pains, sorrows and hell,

They are the things that are keeping me down,

That won't let me win, grow-achieve or excel.

My palms they are callous from lugging this thing.

I must put it down and it has to be now.

I'm tired of the hurt, the guilt and the shame.

I would throw it away if I only knew how.

I carry this bag in spite of myself

I hate it the more, as I watch it grow,

And though it contains both darkness and death

I lug it, I hate it, but it's all that I know.[59]

By Dr. J. Calvin Alberty

There is so much stuff inside of our minds (our mental suitcase) from our past. It is stuff that is reaching out their tentacles controlling and manipulating us as if we were powerless puppets. But we are not powerless. Too many of us are like a picture that I once saw of a monkey with his hand inside a bottle with a narrow neck. The bottle was secured to the ground. It was filled with peanuts. The monkey had to flatten his hand to get it through the narrow opening provided by the neck of the bottle. He then grabbed a hand full of peanuts.

This jar was a trap set by hunters. They approach the monkeys in broad daylight with clubs in their hands. They would use these clubs to strike and kill the monkeys. I know that this sounds harsh and it is, but bear with me. As the hunters approached, the monkeys screamed and hollered and tried to run away. The only thing that held them there was the fact that they would not let go of the peanuts, flatten their hand, withdraw it from the bottle and run. Instead they stood there refusing to let go of the peanuts and were killed.

Listen, there is too much stuff that we are not letting go of. We are either holding onto it or allowing it to hold on to us. It is stuff that is leading us to a similar fate as that of the monkey.

    Let it go! Please let it go and ask God to help make IT let go of you. The problem is that many of us cannot let go of whatever it is, because we no longer know what we're holding onto or what is holding on to us. And many who do know what they are holding onto, do not themselves understand or know why they can't let go of it. This is the case because the "why" is deeply buried and hidden at the unconscious level.

By Dr. J. Calvin Alberty

The Structure of the Mind

So now is a good time to investigate exactly what does unconscious level mean? Think of your mind as an "iceberg"... The conscious mind is the tip of the iceberg riding on and above the surface of the water.

On the other hand, the unconscious mind is the iceberg's enormous segment, lying just under the water's surface level. This is where almost all of our learned behavior... our habits... and our mental schemas reside; within the vast region of the unconscious mind. Allow me to illustrate what I mean with the drawing that is located on the following page.

The conscious mind is the tip of the iceberg that is above the surface of the water. This is the part where we are aware of what is going on in our world. It is where we think, reason, and construct our world to make sense of it. This is where we find what is labeled as intelligence and other cognitive activities. If you will notice that this top part of the iceberg is very small compared to the lower portion.

By Dr. J. Calvin Alberty

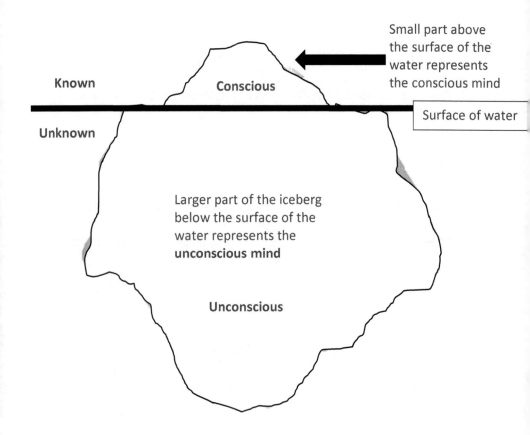

In comparison to the smaller upper portion or conscious, the unconscious mind (THE WHO CAN KNOW IT PART) is the iceberg's huge section that is resting below the surface of the water. Our unconscious is the sum total of our life experiences up to now! That is everything that we have ever experienced in our lives. Everything that we have seen, heard, tasted, felt, smelled, feared, enjoyed, etc. is lodged somewhere in our unconscious.

If we face the reality of our experiences, we have all been exposed to TONS of input ... correct and incorrect; positive and negative; good and bad; just and unjust. We have seen and experienced more than we could ever verbalize or even care to verbalize. For most of us, life is tough. It has never professed to be fair.

According to "The National Science Foundation,[60] Mind-Sets,[61] and LONI (Laboratory of Neuro Imaging),[62] the latter of which is affiliated with the University of Southern California; According to these entities . . . they report that the average number of thoughts that humans are believed to

By Dr. J. Calvin Alberty

experience each day are between 50,000 to 70,000; and 70% of those thoughts are believed to be negative.[63] That means that from 35,000 to 49,000 negative thoughts are bombarding and attacking our minds EVERYDAY. [64]

Raj Raghunathan Ph.D., refers to this by asking the question, "How negative is your "Mental Chatter"? He then posits that . . ."Your sub-conscious thoughts may be more negative than you realize."[65] The article states that even though people claim to hold themselves in high regard, "the thoughts that spontaneously occur to them—their "mental chatter," so to speak—is mostly (up to 70%) negative, a phenomenon that could be referred to as negativity dominance."[66] Deep down in their sub-conscious, about their life. . . it turns out that people are much more self-critical, pessimistic, and fearful than they let out in their conscious thoughts.[67]

The Cleveland Clinic of Wellness, Stress Free Now online article states that "Each person has an average of 60,000 thoughts a day! That's one thought per second in every waking hour! Amazingly, 95 percent are the same thoughts repeated every day. On average, 80 percent of those habitual thoughts are negative. Unfortunately, our brains are hardwired to pay more attention to negative experiences than to positive ones."[68]

The real numbers are really irrelevant. The point that is being made is that we have a "whole-lot-of" negative thoughts at the unconscious level. Many of these thoughts are repetitive in nature. And because of these tons of repetitive negative input and corresponding brain chatter, we are often being steered by negative thoughts that we are not even aware of. It is sort of like what takes place with a ship rudder.

As large as the ship is in proportion to its rudder, which is below the surface of the water, it is that very rudder, as small as it is, that steers the ship. Likewise it is the unconscious thoughts that steer the conscious mind, which steers the person.

By Dr. J. Calvin Alberty

This is what is meant by "We cannot change our hearts (mind), we cannot control our thoughts, our impulses, our affections."[69] Listen, we cannot control them because they are down there on the unconscious level churning away. This is also what is meant by Jeremiah 17:9 when it says, "The HEART is deceitful above all things, and desperately wicked: WHO CAN KNOW IT?" We cannot control it, because it is not accessible to us. In the landscape of full disclosure, I will say this to you, there is a way to find out some of what is there over time. The Bible gives us this method. The subject for "How to know the unconscious mind," will be included in another planned book that will be entitled, "Who Filled My Cup?"

Other Factors Contributing to the Loss of Control

There is another amazing aspect to the brain relative to how we can lose control over our thoughts, impulses, and affections. What if we did not have to think about things that should require thought? What if parts of our brains were short circuited and wired in such a way as to minimize the cognitive or thinking process?

Wouldn't that give Satan a decided advantage over us? Would he not, for every practical and sinister purpose, exploit his advantage to what would be a disadvantage and weakness for us? If such a method existed for circumventing the thought process so that things were more of a reaction than a response, wouldn't that be scary? Regardless of what it would be a reaction to, reacting circumvents thinking, and is probably only good for safety and survival.

This is the first and only time that I will ask you to make an assumption. Let's make this assumption relative to our senses. That assumption is that the reaction that Satan would try to elicit from us, would surely be triggered through one or more of our five senses.

Now after the assumption, let's begin the investigation of this process and take it one step at a time to see if this is in fact the case. The first step is to agree that we have already established that we think with our brain or mind. The second step is to understand that our decisions are usually made with thoughts relative to such things as consequences, pleasure, sought after outcomes (objective or goal oriented), or some other factor that brings pleasure and / or avoids pain.

What if this pleasure could be made to be addictive? What if the addictive substance drove us to become addicts because of the pleasures that we derived from the "seeking out, finding, and using" behaviors? What if we no longer cared about the consequences of our addictive behavior? Further still, what if what we previously had to think about doing became what is essentially an automatic behavior?

Now with this understanding under our belt, let's talk about the reward pathways that we alluded to earlier, though not with any real detail. We will now look at what they are and how they work. Addiction was once thought of only in relationships to drugs. Things have changed. "Now we include addictions to activities such as excessive use of the internet, pornography, shopping, gambling, overeating, and a host of other activities" (Anderson, 2012).[70] In agreement with this principle, Bostwick and Bucci (2008) asserted basically the same thing by saying that "It becomes increasingly clear that a malfunctioning reward center is common to all compulsive behaviors, whether drug abuse, overeating, gambling, or excessive sexual activity."[71] "Recent advances in radiology have demonstrated common pathways within the pleasure center of the brain that "light up" uniquely in people with addictions to either substances or activities." Anderson, Warren (2012) .[72]

All of this is pointing to the fact that there are reward pathways in the brain. They are mostly located in the nucleus accumbens (a location in the brain under the cerebral cortex). "The brain registers all pleasures in the same way, whether they originate with a psychoactive drug, a monetary reward, a sexual encounter, or A SATISFYING MEAL."[73]

Did you get that? It does not matter what the pleasure yielding activity is, the brain sees it all the same way. Dopamine is released to enhance the pleasure that is being experienced around a gratifying activity or substance. This behavior becomes learned because of dopamine's interaction with another neuro transmitter called glutamate. Together, they literally "take over the brain's system of reward-related learning.[74]

These neurotransmitters cause the individuals to link "liking something with wanting it, in turn driving us to go after it. That is, this process motivates us to take action to seek out the source of pleasure."[75] If you ask me, I would say that this is another term for addictive behavior, which "provides a shortcut to the brain's reward system by flooding the nucleus accumbens with dopamine."[76]

In a nutshell, we do something that brings us pleasure; the behavior is repeated until it is learned. We are rewarded by our brain with dopamine, the same as others are with addictive drugs. Because the reward pathway circuitry has been wired for pleasure by these substances (food), now we do not have to think about getting the food. It becomes an automatic response to environmental cues. These reward pathway have become short cuts to the brain's reward center, to which we have become slaves. I did not use this word "slaves" accidentally.

The word addict in its origin means one who is bound, enslaved, sentenced, or condemned. More specifically, they were slaves that were given to Roman soldiers who had done well in battle or service to Rome (Wiktionary).[77] I personally think that enslavement to any substance is, without exception, a sad and wretched condition.

By Dr. J. Calvin Alberty

The New Mindset of Mind Control

Relative to now, the new mindset is that ONLY GOD can know the mind, so only God can reveal it. Only God can know this wickedness and this deceitfulness of the heart that Jeremiah speaks so eloquently of. There is a definitive need for each of us to believe and know that ONLY GOD can do something about the heart of man's sad condition.

We should all be so grateful to God that He has shown us that life without Him is meaningless? Aren't you ecstatic that our loving and compassionate benefactor God is: omniscient, omnipotent, and omnipresent? Because He is omniscient (all-knowing), all the stuff at the unconscious level that is hidden from us is fully in His view.

This is why God says in Proverbs 3:5-6 "Trust in the Lord with all thine heart; and lean not unto thine own understanding. In all thy ways acknowledge him, and he shall direct thy paths." This is also why God says in Proverbs 14:12 "There is a way which seemeth right unto a man, but the end thereof are the ways of death." God tells us this because it is the truth. When I say that only God can know the true condition of the heart, and only our God can do something about it, I mean just that! This is because man only looks at the outside, and he does a very poor job of even doing that.

1 Samuel 16:7 declares, "The Lord seeth not as man seeth; for man looketh on the outward appearance, but the Lord looketh on the heart." It should comfort us to know that because God does look on the heart, and is aware of every problem of the mind, He knows how to help us. He knows where to lead us. He knows how to make a way of escape for us.

Listen, nothing is hidden from Him. He can fix the heart if we will only give him access to it. He is ready to enter the moment that we stop blocking Him and locking Him out. We do this by polluting our minds through poor dietary choices, and by not adhering to the clear laws of health.

Stop for a moment and think about it. With all of the stuff in the unconscious that is steering us, AND having so many negative thoughts, AND encountering so many negative situations AND so many negative people on a daily basis... WE HAVE TO KNOW THAT WE CANNOT MAKE IT WITHOUT GOD'S PRESENCE; AND WITHOUT GOD'S HELP! Here's the skinny on what is being said.

Almost all of the stuff that was placed in our unconscious was put there by other people.

Most of these other people placed the stuff there when we were just young children or teens.

Do you understand what that means? That means that most of what you and I believe is unverified and unfounded. Most of the stuff placed in our unconscious happened when we were much too young to assess it for merit and value.

Do you understand what THAT means? That means that we are living most of our lives based on things that we received and believed as the gospel, from fallible, imperfect and troubled people with mostly negative thoughts. The truth is that many of them had no idea of what their impact would be on us.

By Dr. J. Calvin Alberty

Therefore we end up living our lives based upon FIXATED BELIEFS, which are unproven teachings acquired from our past. These past teachings operate on our lives like skilled surgeons; cutting away who we are, as we live the will of those from our past. We add insult to injury by then trying to live the remainder of our lives in conformity with the biased expectations of those in our present and future world.

This is why our minds must be an open throne-room where God alone rules; because without Him, we have no life of our own. We are merely an extension of those from our past and the expectations of those in our lives today and those who will be in our lives in the future.

Please allow me one more word on these fixated beliefs and then I will gingerly step down from my soapbox. I don't quite remember how I got up on it in the first place, but before I step down, let me add this. All of the stuff from our past that controls us, is effective because, like those subject to the influence of the witch doctor, we came to believe in the magical and unchallenged powers wielded by our past and fear even the thought of changing. The Bible says that God has not given us a spirit of fear, so who is the author of this fear of changing? The enemy is the author. Yet, God reminds us that greater is He that is in us, than he that is in the world. God has already overcome the world. God has already overcome what you fear. ONLY BELIEVE.

By Dr. J. Calvin Alberty

Three Ways We Believe and Hold onto Things

Charles Sander Peirce (1877) said that there were three unscientific ways that we come to believe things (The Fixation of Belief). He called them the: Authority Method; Tenacity Method, and A Priori Method.[78] The Authority Method is when we take someone's word on blind faith. I use the word blind here because we allow ourselves to be blinded because they are in some position of authority or influence. This could be anyone from a teacher, preacher, parent, scout leader, coach, celebrity, etc.

There is another nonscientific method known as "a priori method." This refers to something that is accepted without previous investigation. In the a priori method, if something seems logical and flows in the direction of reason, then it is believed as if it was a certified fact. Remember, they once believed that the earth was the center of the universe and that the earth was flat. How did that turn out?

I personally believe that this last method is the one that is most dangerous to the believer. It is called the method of

By Dr. J. Calvin Alberty

tenacity. This is when a person holds onto something in spite of innumerable volumes of evidence to the contrary. This is the case even if they profess to be a Christian, and you cite one Bible verse after another that contradict their view on a particular subject matter. They unceremoniously dismiss the evidence as they tenaciously hold on to their unfounded, unsupported, baseless and hollow beliefs. This is who they have become, and they are afraid of becoming anything other than what they are. Hmmm, maybe I will call this the "witch doctor effect."

Their lives become ephemeral and non-transitory. They are stuck like glue, while paradoxically being as fleeting as vapor that is blown away without a trace. Like vapor, because they never were anything more than a shadow of others in their past. They never found their purpose, because they were too busy being someone other than themselves. They forever existed in the shallow and rigid experience that they called life. However, life is about living, not a mere existence.

I don't know if they chose one of these three ways, or in their passiveness, fears, or apathy, they allowed one of the three ways to choose them. The ability to think is probably one of the most important gifts ever given to man. However, sometimes when I look around, it seems that it is one of the least appreciated and used gifts. I want to encourage you to continue to be a thinker. There is a quote that I originated some years ago. It is very simple, but it is also very meaningful, and somewhat evocative. It simply says, "The greatest and most inexcusable form of laziness is allowing someone else to think for you."

Obviously, if you have read this book to this point, you are a thinker. Encourage those around you to think outside of "usual." Inspire them to be excited and enthusiastic about believing in unlimited possibilities for themselves. Ralph Waldo Emerson said, "Nothing great has ever been accomplished without enthusiasm." There is so much more that I would like to say to you that would help you breathe the breath of "I can do all things through Christ." I will share with you, one of my favorite writings in this world. I wrote this as my personal philosophy of how to live life. I will share it with you at the end of this book. It is my prayer that it will have a profound effect on you and those that I hope you will share it with. Now, let me move on to the final chapter of this book. Wait a minute, I cannot move on. I have to give you one more example of the method of tenacity.

Do you remember reading a book published in November 1859 called "On the Origin of Species by Means of Natural Selection, or the Preservation of Favoured Races in the Struggle for Life?" If not, maybe you remember its shorter name; "On the Origin of Species." It is a well-known book written by Charles Darwin on the subject of evolutionary biology.

Well do you remember a book called the Bible? The Bible contains 66 books, written by various individuals who were moved by the Spirit of God (2 Peter 1:21, 2 Timothy 3:16). God's book introduces God in this manner, "In the beginning God . . ." (Genesis 1:1). It does not explain His origin, because it says He has none (Genesis 1:1). He always has been and always will be. This book, the Bible lets us know that God is the original Creationist (Genesis 1:1). It say that God created everything that is, and without Him, nothing that has been made was made (John 1:3).

God speaks with absolutes and with absolute authority. There are no conjectures, hypotheses, theories, or speculations. God's book does not waffle or vacillate on anything. The individuals that wrote it were flawed. Some had horrific histories (David). All were sinners. Not one of them professed to be perfect. One even called himself wretched (Paul). Yet, because these flawed individuals were only vessels through which God wrote (2 Timothy 3:16), there is the sweetest harmony between their writings. Most of them never met each other. Some were on different continents and existed in different periods in history. Yet their writings complemented each other in ways that were statistically impossible.

By Dr. J. Calvin Alberty

One said that the earth was round (Isaiah 40:22) and another said that the earth hung on nothing (Job 26:7). Then thousands of years later when man went into outer-space and looked back at the earth, there it was. It was exactly what the Spirit had given to those holy men to write. Now the eyes and cameras of spacemen thousands of years later confirmed the words of the prophets exactly as God had described it. What an amazing God!

God, with no beginning and no end, spoke truth that none can refute with anything other than theories and conjectures. God does not tell us what He thinks or what He believes. He tells us what He knows, what He witnessed, and what He caused to happen.

On the other hand, most men who come up with theories do so with the understanding that they are just that, "theories." Sometimes, because these theories exist for a long period of time, people begin to accept them as fact. It is as if they no longer need to be validated with irrefutable evidence.

Let me define what a theory is for you. It is no more than a presumed knowledgeable explanation of observations based on suppositions relative to a particular topic. A theory is not a fact. In short, it is the best explanation that we have to explain something for right now, until further, scientifically based, knowledge is contraindicative to the point that the previous theory must be modified or abandoned.

With that explained, let me now make a simple statement. Darwin's book entitled "On the Origin of Species" was a book on the THEORY of evolution. His books purports a theory, not a fact. I was curious, as most people who do research are. I began wondering and pondering on how many times did Darwin's book speak on the issue of evolution with uncertainty. You know, I was curious as to how many times did he use words like "suppose," "I believe," and "I think" etc. Here's what I found.

The approximate number of times that each of these words or phrases of uncertainty appear are as follows below.

80 supposed

By Dr. J. Calvin Alberty

55 I believe

245 believe

39 "I think"

55 might be

22 it might

183 could

88 could be

14 it appears

33 infer or infers

134 probably

135 possible or possibly

160 seem or it seems

147 theory

4 theoretical

16 do not know

59 belief

268 should

That's over 1700 words or phrases of uncertainty. Of course there could have been more, I am just too exhausted to look for them outside of using a word search program. Now ask yourself the question, "Can anyone believe this?" When the foundational writer has inserted more than a thousand would-ofs, could-ofs, and should-ofs type of phrases in his writing? I am much more than leery, suspicious or untrusting. I just outright do not believe it. Yet people hold onto Darwin as if he is some type of god, and his writings are unfailing infallible facts. Talking about a method of tenacity, wow.

By Dr. J. Calvin Alberty

A New Mindset Conclusion

Every letter, every period, each dot over an "i" and every slash over each "t" has been written with the purpose of getting you to begin a new mindset relative to your journey to heaven. Beginning a new mindset means thinking about your thinking. Thinking about thinking is known as meta-thinking or meta-cognition. So why do you think the way that you do? Why do you believe what you believe? Instead of asking this question in a broader sense, why not ask this question in a manner which particularly refers to our thoughts on food, and what food symbolizes to you?

For many, many, many years, eating and thinking about food was something I lived and loved to do. Taste was the avenue to my soul that was left unguarded for far too long. I am thankful for grace and mercy. I thank God for His revelation of truth. I also thank God for individuals like Dr. David Moore, M.D., who consistently holds up the banner of health and healthiness as something that God desires for all

By Dr. J. Calvin Alberty

of us. So knowledgeable and so humble, what a rare combination to be found in people nowadays.

Now for the task at hand. We have come to the point of articulating the myriad of things that "Beginning a new mindset" means in regards to the "GOD, AND THE MIND-OF-MAN CONNECTION." Starting a new mindset means:

- Recognizing that there is so much active and dynamic "stuff" in your mind that is circulating and recirculating over and over again and again.
- Understanding that of all of the stuff that is going on at the unconscious level of your mind, is not perceptible to your conscious mind. In fact, though you are not even aware that it is going on, it is steering your every decision.
- Realizing that negative thoughts can be harmful as well as detrimental. It is purported that there are 35,000 - 49,000 of these negative thoughts that are assaulting our minds daily. They are thoughts from which our awareness is disconnected.

- Knowing and appreciating that only God has direct access to these thoughts and our mind. Additionally, it means possessing some level of gratitude for God's desire to protect our minds and effectively deal with these negative thoughts.

- Knowing, that in order for God to do something about our thoughts at the unconscious and conscious levels, He has to be able to communicate with us by way of our minds. Therefore we should be doing everything within our power to let Him in to take up His place of residence in our hearts. This should give us great comfort, because light and darkness cannot coexist. So where Jesus is, the enemy cannot exist.

- Knowing that Satan works through the five senses to access our minds in an effort to dethrone God. Accordingly, we must guard our senses at all times and take seriously the ramifications of leaving these avenues accessible to Satan.

By Dr. J. Calvin Alberty

- Knowing that appetite is one of Satan's main highways to the mind. As a result of this knowledge, we should give special attention to our appetites and the behaviors elicited by food.
- Knowing that though appetite is a major point of entrance, all of the senses are potential doors for Satan to enter and ultimately attack our minds.
- That we must do everything within our power to not only guard the avenues to the mind, but to also be proactive in planning the time, amounts, and frequency of meals.
- Knowing that Satan has no power at all over us, unless we give it to him.
- We must know the importance of feeding our brains and not our taste buds. Feeding the brain properly is feeding the body properly, remember that they are one.

- As you take body and mind's oneness into account, also note that what is bad for the body is bad for the brain/mind.
- That we must remember that Satan declared that he will exalt his throne above the stars of God, and that he would be like the Most High.
- Remembering that ever since iniquity was found in Satan, he has always desired worship.
- Understanding that the throne-room of God, which is where He met with man on earth, was the Most Holy Place; now it is our mind.
- We know that Satan lied about taking the universal throne from God, though he had the audacity to try.
- Knowing that if we do not adhere to God's warning about appetite from His word and His prophetess, then Satan may very well do in our hearts, what he could not and cannot do anywhere else. And that is... Sit on its unholy throne as the god of our bellies.

- We must know that the mind, in the body temple, is the only place that God meets with us; and in that sense, it is therefore akin to the Most Holy Place.
- Finally, beginning a new mindset means understanding that the belly god or flesh god will lead us all down paths to innumerable Christless graves to await the Day of Executory Judgment.

In contrast to this, if we are faithful to the God of love and creation, we will be able to stand in that day and hear the words, "Well done, thou good and faithful servant." The decision has and always will be ours. Like Adam and Eve, with the forbidden fruit and the serpent on one side, and obedience to God on the other side, so are we today. Our forks, spoons, and knives are on one side, and obedience to God is on the other side. The deception is still the same. "Ye shall not surely die." "You're different" It says. "It won't affect you like that because you're special. You are a servant of the Lord. Surely He will not let anything happen to you." Eat, drink and be merry. Not unlike Eve, we give the serpent our attention and listen to the whisperings of his destructive lies to our own demise. We are cursed with living deceived lives, because we do not love the truth of God as much as we do the pleasures that our senses give to us. 2Thessalonians 2:11 "And for this cause God shall send them strong delusion, that they should believe a lie."

God does not deceive us, and nor does He force us to believe His truth. So He allows us to be deceived by the enemy, who we bow to and worship. They are our idols the forks, spoons, and knives. And then we sacrifice our bodies and minds on the altar of our plates as we bow our heads and ask God's blessings on our idolatrous practices.

Let's say good-bye to those practices altogether. Let's accept once and for all, the invitation of Christendom, and that is to be like Jesus. Let us reach out to gain an understanding of Paul's words when he wrote in Philippians 3:13, "Brethren, I count not myself to have apprehended: but this one thing I do, forgetting those things which are behind, and reaching forth unto those things which are before."

By Dr. J. Calvin Alberty

It is time for a new mindset as we embrace the knowledge of the "GOD, AND THE MIND-OF-MAN CONNECTION." That new mindset tells us that if we are willing to give God our five senses, then God will take care of our brain / mind. In fact, let me show you this, God says in James 3:2 "For in many things we offend all. If any man offend not in word, the same is a perfect man, and able also to bridle the whole body." This is saying that if man can control his tongue, he can control his whole body. What if we included the tongue relative to the sense of taste? In other words, what if this meant completely bridling the tongue? That means having full control over what you say and what you eat or drink. So what it is saying is, if we can completely control or tame our tongues, we could win every struggle. However, on our own, we can never do this, as I will discuss in quoting James 3:8 later.

He also says in James 3:6 that the tongue defiles the whole body. We know that among the members of the body of Christ (the church), the tongue defiles the whole body. Now I need you to open your mind here on this point.

Again, what if in its dualistic meaning, this text of scripture also meant that the tongue in the body temple, defiles the whole body? Would that not be in perfect harmony with what we have thus far shown within the context of these writings?

This text reflects the importance of taming the tongue. However, please understand that this is why we must give all of our senses to Jesus and fully recognize that apart from Him we can do absolutely nothing. We cannot even take our next breath in. Even though James 3:8 says, "But the tongue can no man tame; it is an unruly evil, full of deadly poison." It might as well also say that we cannot tame ANY of the senses. We will forever fail, we will forever be victims of Satan until we fully understand the true essence of, and the complementary nature of the following two texts of scripture when they are combined.

By Dr. J. Calvin Alberty

They are Philippian 4:13 and John 15:5. I can do all things through Christ which strengtheneth me, but because I am like a branch that is totally, wholly, and completely dependent upon God for my life and for the ability to produce fruit for the body of Christ; without Jesus, I can do nothing.

This is no less the condition that Jesus was in when He was here on earth. Listen to what He said in John 8:28, "Then said Jesus unto them, When ye have lifted up the Son of man, then shall ye know that I am he, and that I do nothing of myself; but as my Father hath taught me, I speak these things." And in John 5:19 we find these words, "Then answered Jesus and said unto them, Verily, verily, I say unto you, The Son can do nothing of himself, but what he seeth the Father do: for what things soever he doeth, these also doeth the Son likewise."

My final thought is this, to have an awareness and understanding of the "GOD, AND THE MIND-OF-MAN CONNECTION, is worthy of your best efforts. We are coming to a point now in the history of the church and the world, where we will need the greatest clarity ever.

Many will be blinded and lulled into a lukewarm state of existence. They will be shocked when they hear the words of our Lord spoken as written in Matthew 7:23, ". . . I never knew you: depart from me, ye that work iniquity." God loves you. He wants to sit on the throne in the throne room of your mind. Will you allow Him in that He might come in and sup with you, and that you might enjoy what He has prepared for you for all eternity? Give Him the full reigns of your heart / mind, and I can promise you that your life will never again be the same.

By Dr. J. Calvin Alberty

WISDOM

Behold our house, the earth. Observe the family, of man. We are all the seed, of Adam. We are one. We have not made ourselves. Therefore, there is a God; the Creator of all that is good; and the sustainer of all that lives. Be at peace with Him, for He is love. Come to know Him, for He is wisdom. Seek His path, it is truth. See the world around you. In all of its complexity, it is yet simple.

Go beyond the quaint huts by the side of the road and the over populated metropolis. See the people; individual souls in search of happiness. They are the world. And the world can never be any worse or better than you and I. Therefore, we must strive to be ethical.

Fairness must be much more than a philosophy. It must be a way of life. Look within yourself. If you look long enough and deep enough within, you will find a talent and a genius that is unique to you. And if you do not bring it to the table of brotherhood, we are all the lesser because of it.

By Dr. J. Calvin Alberty

Give generously of yourself. With diligence and determination, endeavor to improve the lot of those around you. Sow peace where there is turmoil, love amidst hatred, strength where there is weakness, and joy where there is sorrow.

Give careful thought to your words before they are spoken. For they can easily build or destroy a life. Speak the truth always and in humility. And ever remember, that silence continues to be virtuous. Speak your opinion quietly and rarely. For it is merely that, an opinion.

There are negatives all around you. If focused on, they will rob you of your energy and life force. They will steal your joy and leave you hopeless, avoid them. There are many positives, find them, laugh, it is medicine for your soul.

Your body is a living temple, honor it with: clean water within and without, exercise, a wholesome diet of fruits, nuts, grains, and vegetables, sunshine in moderation, fresh air, meditation to the living God, and a surrendering of all burdens to Him.

Now, love yourself, knowing that you are of great value. For One greater than us all thought enough of you to lay down His life on your behalf. Be calm and do not become unduly disturbed by the affairs of this world. Remember, the world was here before you, and it will be here when you have long departed. It owes you nothing.

Love not temporal things, things that you cannot take with you. Love people, and accept them as they are. Teach chiefly by precepts and examples, for many fools have spoken wisely, but their words have gone unheeded because they did not equate to their lifestyle.

Your words will have a far reaching influence when paired with your deeds. You were not born with a gavel in your hand. Nor do you possess infinite wisdom. Accordingly, judge no one, for you have but one narrow perspective, your own.

Carefully put on the moccasins of others and walk lightly in their paths. Put on their glasses and see their world. Implant within your bosom, their hearts, and feel their pain. I

By Dr. J. Calvin Alberty

can assure you, the world will never be the same to you again. There remains a question that each person must answer of themselves. "Is the world a better place as a result of my having been here?" Look long and pensively into the mirror. Do you love the person you see? Evolve! Change! Become and grow, until you are in love with yourself.

There are no limits, boundaries or barriers that you cannot surpass if you dare open your mind to possibilities. Look above you at the heavens in all of their celestial splendor, the stars, the moon and the sun. Behold the vastness of the universe. With all of its endless depth, breadth and height, there remains no room for hate, ignorance and injustice.

Though we are many languages, many colors, and many cultures and ethnic diversities, still and always, we are one race---HUMAN! And among humans, there is no beauty above love. And from love emanates forgiveness, tolerance, mercy, compassion, kindness and charity. Therefore be beautiful, like the perennial grass speckled with flowers upon a rolling meadow, be beautiful. Like the sun garbed in its radiance as it sets beyond the endless sea, be beautiful.

We are billions upon the face of one earth! It is the household of man. A house divided against itself, cannot stand! There is but one earth. It cannot be divided. Therefore, we must love each other, and those who have lost the capacity to love, as unfortunate as they are, at the very least they must tolerate each other.

Whatever problem might confront the family of man, love remains the solution. Therefore, love God, love yourself, love others and love life. For the day that you stop loving, you stop living. THIS IS WISDOM![79]

By Dr. J. Calvin Alberty

NOTES

1. All scriptures quoted within the context of this book are from the King James Version of the Holy Bible unless otherwise specified.

2. Any words capitalized, underscored, bolded, within any quotations were added by the author for the purpose of emphasis and were not a part of the original document being quoted.

3. Just in case you did not know, when you see a super script number behind a statement like this "[7]", this number [7] seven, means that you can look under the references in the back of this book and look at the reference that is numbered 7 and it will tell you that what you just read came from the source that is listed by the seventh entry under the reference list, which is:

7. Morgan, J. (2015). Exploring the mind: Still so much to map out. The Lancet Neurology, 14(2), 143. doi:http://dx.doi.org/10.1016/S1474-4422(14)70236-4

By Dr. J. Calvin Alberty

References

1. Merriam-Webster online dictionary

2. The Temporal Dynamics of Learning Center, University of California at San Diego.

3. US National Library of Medicine National Institutes of Health, Normal weight of the brain in adults in relation to age, sex, body height and weight Hartmann P1, Ramseier A, Gudat F, Mihatsch MJ, Polasek W.

4. Smithsonian Institute National Museum of Natural History 10/25/2015. http://humanorigins.si.edu/human-characteristics/brains.

5. Ibid

6. Lewis, Tanya. Human Brain: Facts, Anatomy & Mapping Project. Live Science. March 26, 2015.

7. Morgan, J. (2015). Exploring the mind: Still so much to map out. The Lancet Neurology, 14(2), 143. doi:http://dx.doi.org/10.1016/S1474-4422(14)70236-4

8. Ibid

9. Begley DJ, and Brightman MW. Structural and functional aspects of the blood–brain barrier. Prog Drug Res. 2003;61: pp. 39–78.

10. Brain proteome response following whole body exposure of mice to mobile phone or wireless DECT base radiation; Adamantia F. Fragopoulou , Athina Samara , Marianna H. Antonelou , Anta Xanthopoulou , Aggeliki Papadopoulou , Konstantinos Vougas , Eugenia Koutsogiannopoulou , Ema Anastasiadou , Dimitrios J. Stravopodis , George Th. Tsangaris , Lukas H. Margaritis Electromagnetic Biology and Medicine Vol. 31, Iss. 4, 2012

11. LONI, Laboratory of Neuro Imaging http://www.loni.usc.edu/about_loni/education/brain_trivia.php

12. Shrimathi Swaminathan on 26 April 2014 Posted in Lifestyle and Behaviour, The Human Brain.

13. Bourre, J. M. (2006). Effects of nutrients (in food) on the structure and function of the nervous system: update on

dietary requirements for brain. Part 2: macronutrients. The Journal of Nutrition, Health & Aging, 10(5), 386-99. Retrieved from http://search.proquest.com/docview/222241003?accountid=38769

14. Bernard B. Brodie and Parkhurst A. Shore; A concept for a role of serotonin and norepinephrine as chemical mediators in the brain. 15 DEC 2006, DOI: 10.1111/j.1749-6632.1957.tb40753.

15. Arteriosclerosis, Thrombosis, and Vascular Biology. 2004; 24: 806-815 Published online before print February 5, 2004, doi: 10.1161/01.ATV.0000120374.59826.1b

16. Elsevier B.V., Intelligence, Volume 41, Issue 6, November–December 2013, Pages 843–850, doi:10.1016/j.intell.2013.04.006,

17. Source: National Center for Biotechnology Information, U.S. National Library of Medicine, The Associated Press Research Date: April 2nd, 2015

18. Cell Press. (2011, August 3). Why diets don't work: Starved brain cells eat themselves, study finds. ScienceDaily. Retrieved October 11, 2015 from www.sciencedaily.com/releases/2011/08/110802125546.htm

19. Daniel Amen, M.D. CEO, Amen Clinics, Inc. Distinguished Fellow, American Psychiatric Association http://www.solutionresources.net/The_Incredible_Brain_-D_Amen-.pdf

20. The White Estate, Inc. http://www.whiteestate.org/about/egwbio.asp

21. White, E. Special Testimonies on Education, pg. 33. C1917.

22. White, E. Child Guidance, pg. 446.

23. Centers for Disease Control and Prevention. Recommendations to improve preconception health and health care—United States. MMWR Recommendations and Reports. 2006;55(RR-06):1–23

24. Dezfouli, A., & Balleine, B. W. (2012). Habits, action sequences and reinforcement learning. European Journal of Neuroscience, 35(7), 1036-1051. doi:http://dx.doi.org/10.1111/j.1460-9568.2012.08050.x

25. Ibid

26. American Psychiatric Association. (2000). Diagnostic and statistical manual of mental disorders (4th ed., text rev.). Washington, DC: Author

27. White, E. Child Guidance, pg. 446.

28. Ibid

29. White, E. Prophets and Kings. pg. 488-489, 1917.

30. Ibid pg. 489, 1917.

31. White, E. Desire of Ages. Pg. 125.

32. Ibid

33. White, E. Adventist Home. Pg. 401.

34. Ibid

35. Ibid

36. Ibid

37. White, E. Christ's Object Lessons pg. 346, 1900.

38. Dezfouli, A., & Balleine, B. W. (2012). Habits, action sequences and reinforcement learning. European Journal of Neuroscience, 35(7), 1036-1051. doi:http://dx.doi.org/10.1111/j.1460-9568.2012.08050.x

39. White, E. Adventist Home. Pg. 401.

40. White, E. Third Volume of the Testimonies, pg. 487, 1875.

41. White, E. & White, J. Christian Temperance and Bible Hygiene. Pg. 487, 1890.

42. Ibid, Pg. 37

43. White, E. Letter 17, 1895; Counsels on Diet and Foods, pg. 138. 23r.

44. Tomm, Sara; Healthy Eating, Five Reasons the Body Needs Energy, Demand Media, http://healthyeating.sfgate.com/five-reasons-body-needs-energy-4673.html

45. The American Journal of Clinical Nutrition, January 2003, Vol. 77, no.1, pg. 91-100.

46. White, E. Health Reformer, May 1877; Counsels on Diet, pg. 181. Mind, Character and Personality, Vol. 2, pg. 443.

47. White, E. Ministry of Healing, pg. 241.

48. Ibid

49. Ibid

50. 46. White, E. Mind, Character and Personality, Vol. 2, pg. 380.

51. White, E. Desire of Ages, pg. 125.

52. Gosnell, B. A., & Levine, A. S. (2009). Reward systems and food intake: Role of opioids. International Journal of Obesity, 33, S54-8. doi:http://dx.doi.org/10.1038/ijo.2009.73

53. White, E. Ministry of Healing, pg. 176, 1905.

54. Harvard Health Blog entitled Unconscious or Subconscious? The article is written by Michael Craig Miller, M.D., Senior Editor, Mental Health Publishing, Harvard Health Publication. The article was posted August 01, 2010.

55. Harvard Health Blog entitled Unconscious or Subconscious? The article is written by Michael Craig Miller, M.D., Senior Editor, Mental Health Publishing, Harvard Health Publication. The article was posted August 01, 2010.

56. 1.Corsini, R. J., & Wedding, D. (2011). Current psychotherapies (9th ed.). Belmont, CA: Brooks/Cole.

57. White, E. Ministry of Healing, pg. 176, 1905.

58. Online Hebrew Lexicon https://www.blueletterbible.org/lang/lexicon/lexicon.cfm?Strongs=h3824&t=KJV

59. The Poetry of Our Lives, Another Voice Book 3, J. Calvin Alberty, 2013.

60. The National Science Foundation, 4201 Wilson Boulevard, Arlington, Virginia 22230, USA

61. Mind-sets.com, 2015.

62. LONI, Laboratory of Neuro Imaging http://www.loni.usc.edu/about_loni/education/brain_trivia.php

63. Ibid

64. Ibid

65. Raghunathan, R. Psychology Today, How Could We Gain Control Over our Negative Mental Chatter? Oct 10, 2013. htttps://www.psychologytoday.com/.../how-negative-is...

66. Ibid

67. Ibid

68. Ibid

69. White, E. Ministry of Healing, pg. 176, 1905.

70. Anderson, Warren E,M.D., M.A. (2012). Addiction and virtue: Beyond the models of disease and choice. Ethics & Medicine, 28(3), 124-125. Retrieved from http://search.proquest.com/docview/1170931427?accountid=38769

71. Bostwick, J. M., & Bucci, J. A., M.D. (2008). Internet sex addiction treated with naltrexone. Mayo Clinic Proceedings, 83(2), 226-30. Retrieved from

http://search.proquest.com/docview/216877758?accountid=38769

72. Anderson, Warren E, M.D., M.A. (2012). Addiction and virtue: Beyond the models of disease and choice. Ethics & Medicine, 28(3), 124-125. Retrieved from http://search.proquest.com/docview/1170931427?accountid=38769

73. Harvard Health Publication, Harvard Medical School. http://www.health.harvard.edu/newsletter_article/how-addiction-hijacks-the-brain

74. Ibid

75. Ibid

76. Ibid

77. Wiktionary

http://english.stackexchange.com/questions/130423/etymology-of-addict

78. Charles Sanders Peirce, "The Fixation of Belief," Popular Science Monthly, November 1877, pp. 1-15.

By Dr. J. Calvin Alberty

https://archive.org/stream/popularsciencemo12newy#page/n9/mode/2up

79. The Poetry of Our Lives, Another Voice Book 3, J. Calvin Alberty, 2013.

Made in the USA
Charleston, SC
12 November 2015